SpringerBriefs in Law

More information about this series at https://link.springer.com/bookseries/10164

Marco Antonio Jiménez Sánchez

The Ultra Vires Doctrine in Corporate Law

A Comparative Review

Springer

Marco Antonio Jiménez Sánchez
Universidad Militar Nueva Granada
Bogotá, Colombia

ISSN 2192-855X ISSN 2192-8568 (electronic)
SpringerBriefs in Law
ISBN 978-3-030-88837-4 ISBN 978-3-030-88838-1 (eBook)
https://doi.org/10.1007/978-3-030-88838-1

This Springer imprint is published by the registered company Springer Nature Switzerland AG
The registered company address is: Gewerbestrasse 11, 6330 Cham, Switzerland

Contents

Abbreviations

ADHGB	Allgemeines Deutsche Handelsgesetzbuch
AG	Aktiengesellschaft
AktG	Aktiengesetz
art.	Article
bG	Bergrechtliche Gewerkschaft
BGB	Bürgerliches Gesetzbuch
C.C.	Civil Code
C.Co.	Commercial Code
CA	Companies Act
Cf.	Confer
Ch.	Chapter
CJI	Inter-American Juridical Committee
Coord.	Coordinador
e.g.	Exempli gratia (for example)
EC	European Community
EEC	European Economic Community
et al.	Et alia (and others)
et seq.	Et sequentes (and what follows)
etc.	Et cetera (and the others)
EU	European Union
GmbH	Gesellschaft mit beschränkter Haftung
GmbHG	Gesetz betreffend die Gesellschaften mit beschränkter Haftung
HGB	Handelsgesetzbuch
i.e.	Id est (that is)
Ibid.	Ibidem (in the same place)
In re	In the matter of
J.	Journal
L.	Law
Lit.	Literal
Ltda.	Sociedad de Responsabilidad Limitada
MBCA	Model Business Corporation Act

MGLC	Mexican General Law of Corporations of 1934
Nat'l	National
Num.	Numeral
OAS	Organization of American States
op. cit.	Opere citato (the work cited)
par.	Paragraph
Pt.	Part
Q.	Quarterly
Rev.	Review
s.	Section
S.A.	Sociedad Anónima
SAS	Société par Actions Simplifiée
SE	Societas Europaea
SPA	Società per Azioni
SRL	Società a Responsabilità Limitata
t.	Tome
tit.	Title
UCC	Uniform Commercial Code
UK	United Kingdom
UNCITRAL	United Nations Commission on International Trade Law
USA	United States of America
Vid.	Vide (see)
Vol.	Volume
Vs.	Versus (against)

Chapter 1
What Is the Ultra Vires Doctrine?

Abstract In this chapter, we do address two issues. Firstly, we answer the question: What is the ultra vires doctrine? In doing so, an explanation of the meaning in corporate law is delivered taking as the starting point the capacity as an attribute of the corporate personality. On the other hand, a brief description of this book's contents is outlined. That way we present the three main thematic axes, which are split up into nine chapters.

1.1 Introduction: What Is the Ultra Vires Doctrine?

According to Black's Law Dictionary ultra vires means: "Unauthorized; beyond the scope of power allowed or granted by a corporate charter or by law".[1] Nevertheless, Machen delivered the following definition: "In its proper sense, it [ultra vires] denotes some act or transaction on the part of a corporation which, although not unlawful or contrary to public policy if done or executed by an individual, is yet beyond the legitimate powers of the corporation as they are defined by the statutes under which it is formed or which apply to it, or by its charter or incorporation paper".[2] There is also a division among authorities regarding the use of the phrase ultra vires to describe acts that are illegal in the sense of being *malum per se* and *malum prohibitum*. It seems that it would be better to use these words to describe only such contracts of corporations exceeding their corporate powers.[3]

---

[1] Garner (2009), p. 1662.

[2] Machen (1908), p. 819. The expression "ultra vires" had already been used by ancient equity scholars in the field of contract law, a long time ago before it was applied to the law of corporations. For instance, "(...) a *bona fide* transaction with a putative proprietor. Such transaction is void at common law as ultra vires; and were there no remedy in equity, the paying debt to a putative creditor would not be more hazardous, than transactions with a putative proprietor. (...)". Cf. Kames (1825), p. 350.

[3] Elliott (1911) §200. However, in Central Transportation Co. v. Pullman Palace Car Co., 139 U.S. 24 (1890) the Court emphasized that: "A contract of a corporation which is ultra vires in the proper sense, that is to say, outside the object of its creation as defined in the law of its organization, and therefore beyond the powers conferred upon it by the legislature is not voidable only, but wholly

M. A. Jiménez Sánchez, *The Ultra Vires Doctrine in Corporate Law*,
SpringerBriefs in Law, https://doi.org/10.1007/978-3-030-88838-1_1

It is correct to assert that ultra vires acts or transactions do not necessarily involve either unlawful or illegal behavior. The act or transaction could be performed by the company because it is in their ambit of competency or business field, but such power to execute or to get involved in the particular affair was not contemplated at the time of the foundation.[4] To sum up this introductory approach: "The doctrine of ultra vires is, that all acts of a corporation, not within the powers conferred upon it by its charter, or the statutes under which it was instituted, or reasonably implied therefrom, are null and void, and as to such acts the corporation may be restrained in equity by an injunction, or it may set up the plea of ultra vires as a defense to an action at law (...) The question whether a particular act of a corporation is ultra vires is determined by a construction of its constating instruments. If the act is prohibited, or against public policy, it is not ultra vires, it is illegal".[5]

Because of this, it is equivocal to hold that in the case of a stock exchange trader who negotiates non-existent securities on behalf of the corporation, that it would thereby be viable to file a suit against the firm due to such an illegal ultra vires act committed by one of their subordinates.[6] Under this hypothesis, there is no room for the ultra vires doctrine, and neither can there be an assertion that such behavior is an exception to an ultra vires act because the corporation cannot plea the ineffectiveness of the acts performed by their employees beyond the limits of the granted powers. In this case, an action at law could be raised on the grounds of a tort.

The ultra vires doctrine is principally concerned with corporations only pursuing the purposes for which they were created, and any kind of act or transaction beyond that point becomes ultra vires, and consequently, void. In other words, if the corporation tries to effect purposes other than those for which it was created, its acts or transactions will be ultra vires and void. Another subsequent variant of the doctrine

void and of no legal effect (...) A contract ultra vires being unlawful and void, not because it is in itself immoral but because the corporation, by the law of its creation, is incapable of making it (...)". According to this line of authority, a distinction must be made: the contracts which are merely unauthorized by the corporate charter are ultra vires, and contracts that are illegal because they are contrary to law, are both ultra vires and illegal.

[4] Nevertheless, at an early stage of the ultra vires doctrine, British courts held in Bagshaw v. Eastern Union Ry. (1850) 2. M. & G. 389: "The Legislature may have thought it right to provide that the capital raised for a specific purpose should not be applied for any other purpose. Under such a state of things, the application of capital so appropriated to any other than the specified purpose must be *unlawful*. No majority of the shareholders, however large, could sanction the misapplication of such a portion of the capital. Indeed, in strictness, even unanimity would not make such an act lawful" (italics added).

In accordance with the opinion of the United States Supreme Court Justice Gray, everybody who deals with a corporation is charged with constructive notice of its powers. An ultra vires act is an illegal act. Therefore A, when he participated in the act, was *particeps criminis*. In re St. Louis Railroad v. Terre Haute Railroad, 145 U.S. 393. See, Warren (1910), p. 507. We are adherents to Professor Warren who claims that this is a ferocious doctrine. Unauthorized corporate action, simply because it is unauthorized, cannot with any propriety be said to be criminal. It is not even illegal if that adjective is used to connote something particularly reprehensible, and not simply to connote something contrary to law. Ibid.

[5] Swaney (1883), p. 2.

[6] Martínez (2007), p. 39, et seq.

teaches that the company's directors have confined powers granted in the articles of association and legal provisions. Therefore, when the directors perform an act or transaction for which they do not have authority, for example, hiring a lawyer or exceeding the power granted them as such to get a bank loan for an amount of money above and beyond what the company's recorded articles of incorporation authorize them to borrow,[7] both become ultra vires.[8] In this writing, we will use the word *director* in its broadest sense to mean any kind of individual, who has been designated by law or appointed by the stockholders to exercise the firm's management.[9]

Ballantine notices that the ultra vires doctrine had its origin in a judicial deduction from the fictional conception of corporations as artificial persons, creatures of the law, which have no existence, powers, or capacity except those granted by statute.[10] Hence a contract made in the name of the corporation for purposes not included in the articles, although by the authority of all the directors, and even with the consent of all the stockholders, has been held by some courts to be unattributable to the corporation at all. The earlier English cases originating the ultra vires doctrine were cases where the only parties concerned were stockholders and the corporation, holding that a minority could restrain the firm from acting outside the purposes provided for. In 1860, the doctrine was extended to relations with third parties. By this extension, it became possible for corporations to evade liability to an irksome contract by showing their actual incapacity to even make the contract.[11]

The ultra vires doctrine has an intimate connection to the company's capacity as an attribute of its personality.[12] Through it, the firms can interact in litigation

[7] Elliott (1911) §212, footnote 48. In this case, the bank can collect only the amount, which the corporation is thus authorized to contract indebtedness for. In re First Nat. Bank V. Kiefer Milling Co., 95 Ky. 97, 23 S. W. 675, 15 Ky. L. 457; First Nat. Bank v. American Nat. Bank, 173 Mo. 153, 72 S. W. 1059; Monument Nat. Bank v. Globe Works, 101 Mass. 57, 3 Am. 322; Lyon, etc., Co. v. First Nat. Bank, 85 Fed. 120, 29 C. C. A. 45; Connecticut River Say. Bank v. Fiske, 60 N. H. 363; Prospect Worsted Mill, 126 Fed. 1011.

[8] Comparative law scholars such as Pistor (2002), p. 818, claims that directors overstepping the established boundaries were acting ultra vires. Then, transactions ultra vires were null and void and directors could be held personally responsible. The success of the ultra vires doctrine as an instrument to control management has had mixed results.

[9] For example, in Colombia the Law 222 of 1995, art. 22, conceived a broad concept of *managers*. Accordingly, the representatives, liquidators, factors, members of the board of directors, and in general anyone that according to the articles of incorporation holds the inherent duties to those positions, are considered as *directors*. In the opinion of the Minister of Justice and the Superintendence of Companies, this is a restrictive enumeration because both the punishable regime and liability involved cannot apply to those individuals not listed in such provision. Therefore, it is not allowed to make an extensive interpretation. Cf. Ministerio de Justicia (1998), p. 143.

[10] Ballantine (1930), pp. 235, 238.

[11] Ballantine (1930), pp. 235, 238.

[12] Geldart (1927), p. 104, holds that to say that all legal personality (natural or juristic) is equally real because the law gives it an existence, and equally artificial or fictitious because it is only the law which gives it an existence, is really confounding *personality* with *capacity*. Despite this author not pointing out the difference between these two legal concepts (personality/capacity) there is a gender to species ratio. The *capacity* is an attribute of the *personality* through which a natural individual or juristic person such as a corporation, may enforce the fulfillment of an obligation or exercise

settings suing and being sued, and in the business environment enforcing obligations and demanding rights. It is obvious that corporations have no physical existence, therefore cannot be perceived through the senses[13]; however, corporations have a legal existence in terms of the law, and its directors on their behalf, may enforce the rights and honor the obligations of the company as if it was the very company doing it. Certainly, the incorporation of a firm is one of the most notorious advances in corporate law because it allows a fictitious entity to enter into the commercial world with legal prerogatives such as being able to contest unlawful behaviors from its competitors before the courts and making it possible to get the necessary goods and services through any contract to perform its object clause broadly.[14]

In turn, in the opinion of Ferrara, the Italian scholar pioneering the analysis of juristic persons, the capacity of juristic persons has been restricted to their patrimony, reducing these moral entities as well by claiming they were machines that only function for such limited ends.[15] Thus, there are expansive or reductionist theories enacted both in legislature and academia. In this way, common law recognizes the ultra vires theory as a juristic person simply acting so as to reach their goals. In that respect, the granted powers do not go beyond those listed in the incorporation memoranda and everything beyond that is nullity and void. An analogous principle to the ultra vires doctrine is still valid in French law: the principle of specialty (*spécialité statutaire*). Thus, in such a country, moral persons are recognized only by their compliance with specific functions. Therefore, their activities are circumscribed toward such an end and outside that mission, there is no personality.[16]

It is instructive the following narrative of Young:

> In commercial associations where the object of the firm is private gain and not public welfare, the substratum of natural persons is more apparent than in any other class of juristic person. It must accordingly be noted that in virtue of these circumstances, they need no special authorization to entitle them to exercise their functions; and that the reasons which make it legitimate for a state arbitrarily to refuse to admit other juristic persons to the exercise of functional capacity do not apply to them. Functional capacity should therefore always be conceded to them, but it is nevertheless open to any state to impose restrictions upon the concession so long as those restrictions are confined to provisions for the protection of the interests of third parties, the subjects of the state, and do not seek to affect the constitution

---

a legal right. In turn, there is a clear distinction between "passive" capacity and "active" capacity adjudicated in re Earl of Shrewsbury v. North Staffordshire Ry. Co. (1865). Cf. Schlink (1935), p. 64. More details about this topic in comparative law, see Harris (2006) *passim*. Research about the nature of legal persons in comparison between common law and civil law, in particular, the four predominant theses in Wolff (1938), pp. 496–505.

[13] Pollock (1911), p. 235 argues: "... the difficulty of ascribing wrongful intention to an artificial person was in truth only a residue of anthropomorphic imagination". A detailed research in France, Audinet (1950) and, in Italy, Verrucoli (1964).

[14] About the meaning of corporate personality and its different theories, in Clark (1986) §16. It is expedient to consider the following elements as required for the existence of a 'corporate juristic person': (a) plurality of individuals; (b) cooperation; (c) organization; (d) exclusive patrimonial capacity; (e) corporate purpose. *Vid.* De Benito (n/d), p. 42. The technical development of the corporate personality from a Latin American civil law context, in Pinzón (1980), pp. 31–44.

[15] Ferrara (1929), p. 778.

[16] Ferrara (1929), p. 778.

and character of the juristic person or the relations of its members *inter se*. The latter must be left to the personal law, and exact from a foreign commercial association the performance of conditions precedent to exercise its functions which would affect its internal constitution, would be improper to disregard its personal law, and practically to deny it personal status.

The function of a commercial association is to carry out some business, and its functional capacity is its capacity to carry out business. When a state imposes upon foreign commercial associations conditions precedent to the enjoyment by them of a right to carry out business, it follows from what has been said that not all foreign commercial associations which desire to perform any act in the law within the territories of that state must necessarily perform the conditions precedent before doing so, or that any act in the law performed by a foreign commercial association that has not performed the conditions precedent is necessarily avoided or otherwise affected by the non-performance. Whether the performance of such an act does or does not amount to carrying on of a business is a question of fact".[17]

Despite corporate personality being a precious legal tool, sometimes it is used to cheat both the law and creditors' rights. It is possible to conceive of fraudulent conduct when the outcome that is prohibited by law, is obtained through an alternate manner otherwise not contemplated in the contravened provision. Justly, law has tried to avoid in a general way such a result, instead of merely prohibiting it allowing the use of another legal device. The law or the contract might be cheated through a juristic person created for such ends, or in abuse of an existing one.[18] Therefore, where a corporation is organized to perpetrate a fraud, the courts have ruled that they will look beyond the corporate unit to the persons who are responsible for its existence.[19]

1.2 Scope of the Text

The text is formed of three main sections divided into nine chapters. The first part (this chapter and Chap. 2) explains what the ultra vires doctrine in the field of corporate law is, following a conceptual presentation of such a doctrine, beginning with its historical backgrounds. A complete analysis of this doctrine is presented next, and

[17] Young (1912), pp. 86–87.

[18] Serick (1958), p. 44. This author also deals with fraudulent conduct employing corporate personality that causes harmful outcomes to the individuals, firms, and third parties, especially, in unfair competition issues linked to contract relationships. Cf. §4, ibid. A comprehensive analysis of this subject matter in the UK and USA from an Italian perspective, in Verrucoli (1964), Chaps. 2–4. For a critical view about the concept of a juristic person in a comparative perspective. See, De Castro (1991) pp. 115–135.

[19] Bank of Chicago v. Trebein Co., 59 Ohio St. 316, 52 N. E. 834 (1898). In this case, courts ignore the entity concept when used as a shield for attempts to swindle creditors. Verrucoli (1964), 46–47, points out that *incorporation* is a privilege that cannot be abused, and those acts executed in that manner must be outlawed or at least, modified through a special act or a general provision. Therefore, the contractual theory of the firm is a counterpart to the idea of corporate personality as an absolute privilege.

finally, an answer to the question whether the ultra vires doctrine should be discarded at all is given.

The second block (Chaps. 3–5) covers the ultra vires doctrine in corporate law from three different angles: common law, European civil law, and Latin America. Taking into account that this doctrine was born in the so-called "origin common law jurisdictions", an exposition of case law and legislative provisions in the United States and the United Kingdom is introduced. We teach then the way that such a doctrine has colonized Australian corporate law, and its subsequent developments. In the next chapter, we examine the influence of the doctrine in the main civil law jurisdictions (France, Germany, Italy, and Spain), and the current application in accordance with the kind of corporation. Finally, a comprehensive study is conducted in the so-called "transplanted" legal systems of modern Latin American jurisdictions (Argentina, Brasil, Colombia, México, and Perú).

The third and final research set (Chaps. 6–8) delves into three key aspects related to the studied doctrine: the objects clause as the purpose and range of activities for which the company is carried on, the legal procedures to reject ultra vires acts and transactions in both civil law and common law jurisdictions, and the legal mechanisms to ratify such kinds of ultra vires acts and transactions when possible, with the help of either judicial or administrative tools.

Lastly, the most relevant conclusions are exposed to the aim of inviting the reader to elaborate his own opinion about the ultra vires doctrine in corporate law.

References

Ballantine H (1930) Manual of corporation law, Chicago
Clark R (1986) Corporate law, New York
De Castro F (1991) Persona Jurídica, Madrid
Elliott C (1911) The law of private corporations, Indianapolis
Ferrara F (1929) Teoría de las Personas Jurídicas, Madrid
Garner B (2009) Black's law dictionary, St. Paul
Geldart W (1927) Elements of English law, London
Harris R (2006) The transplantation of legal discourse on corporate personality theories. Wash Lee L Rev 63:1422
Kames H (1825) Principles of equity, Edinburgh
Machen A (1908) Treatise on the modern law of corporations, vol 2, Boston
Martínez F (2007) Actos Ultra Vires y Protección de la Apariencia Jurídica, México
Ministerio de Justicia (1998) Impacto de la Ley 222 de 1995, Bogotá
Pinzón G (1980) Personificación Jurídica de las Sociedades, Bogotá
Pistor K et al (2002) Evolution of corporate law. U Pa J Int Econ L 23:791
Pollock (1911) Theory of corporations in common law. L Q Rev 27
Schlink C (1935) Die Ultra Vires Lehre im Englischen Privatrecht, Berlin
Serick R (1958) Apariencia y Realidad en las Sociedades Mercantiles, Barcelona
Swaney H (1883) Essay on ultra vires, Washington
Verrucoli P (1964) Superamento della Personalità Giuridica delle Società di Capitali nella Common Law e nella Civil Law, Milano
Warren E (1910) Executed ultra vires transactions. Harvard L Rev 23

Wolff M (1938) On the nature of legal persons. L Q Rev 54:494
Young H (1912) Foreign companies and other corporations, Cambridge

Chapter 2
Conceptual Presentation of the Ultra Vires Doctrine

Abstract In this chapter, we will chronicle the historical backgrounds involved in the development of the ultra vires doctrine, then we make a comprehensive research about such a doctrine in corporate law, commencing with the distinction between a natural person and one of statutory creation, in relation to their capacity as an attribute of its personality. Subsequently, we explain the concept of an ultra vires act and transaction, the scope, legal consequences, and criticism in the main common law and civil law jurisdictions. Finally, an answer to the question concerning its usefulness is submitted.

2.1 Historical Background

It is instructive to chronicle some historical backgrounds of the ultra vires doctrine because like many other juristic institutions in common law, it comes into play when the courts adjudicate cases involving corporate law matters in connection with the exercise of the director's powers, and consequently corporate capacity. It has been typically reffered to *Head v. Providence Ins. Co.*, 2 Oranch, 127 (1804) where the principles which support the defense of ultra vires for unauthorized acts of corporations were first enunciated by the Supreme Court of the United States.[1] In that case, an action was brought regarding two insurance policies taken out on merchandise onboard Spanish brigs which subsequently was lost and destroyed. The Supreme Court uttered as follows:

---

[1] Reese (1897) §21; Swaney (1883), ps. 3–4. According to Holdsworth (1922), p. 398, corporations hold their powers and capacities subject to what in later law will be known as the ultra vires doctrine. The germs both of the law as to the powers and capacities naturally incident to a corporation, and of the supplementary ultra vires doctrine has been implicit in the law from an early period. Both began to be developed during the seventeenth and eighteenth centuries, but they were not as yet highly developed. It would not be until the nineteenth century that ultra vires doctrine developed into a large body of complex rules; and then it would be in relation rather to new statutory corporations than to these older common law corporations. Even at the inception of the twentieth century, the application of the doctrine to the powers of these common law corporations would give rise to some legal problems to which the authorities would give no very certain answer.

M. A. Jiménez Sánchez, *The Ultra Vires Doctrine in Corporate Law*, SpringerBriefs in Law, https://doi.org/10.1007/978-3-030-88838-1_2

> Without ascribing to this body, which, in its corporate capacity, is the mere creature of the act to which it owes its corporate existence, all the qualities and disabilities annexed by the common law to the ancient institutions of this sort, it may correctly be said to be precisely, what the incorporating act has made it, to derive all its powers from that act and be capable of exercising its faculties only in the manner which that act authorizes. With these bodies which have only a legal existence, the act of incorporation is an enabling act. It gives them all the powers they possess. It enables them to contract; and when it prescribes to them a mode of contracting, they must observe that mode, or the instrument no more creates a contract than if the body had never been incorporated.

A few years later in subsequent cases, the Supreme Court decided some legal matters with respect to public utilities,[2] banking,[3] negotiable instruments,[4] sureties,[5] transportation,[6] and contracts[7] applying ultra vires principles. However, Reese considers that the very first case where the ultra vires doctrine was directly considered was *Pearce v. Madison & Indiana B. Co.* decided in 1858.[8] It was there held that two corporations chartered by the state of Indiana to construct and manage distinct though connecting railroads had no power to consolidate themselves into one corporation or to establish a steamboat line on the Ohio river to be run in connection with the railroad, and, therefore, were not liable on a promissory note sued on, which had been given by the officers of the consolidated line in payment of a steamboat.

For more than two centuries, corporate (or company)[9] law has represented the most dynamic and broadest branch of research in commercial law, unlike any other

---

[2] Commonwealth of Pennsylvania v. Philadelphia Electric Co., 18 Pa. Corp. Rep. 243 (1929). In this case, the court said that the sale by the respondent of electrical refrigerators and other electrical appliances is in furtherance of its main corporate purpose of supplying light, heat, and power by electricity to the public, in the territory covered by the respondent's charter.

[3] People v. Utica Ins. Co., 15 John. 357 (1818); Bank of the United States v. Dandridge, 12 Wheat. 64 (1827).

[4] New York Firemen, Ins. Co. v. Sturges, 2 Cow. 664 (1824); Bank of Augusta v. Earle, 13 Pet. 519 (1839); Monument National Bank v. Globe Works, 101 Mass. 57 (1869); Franklin Co. v. Lewiston Ins. for Savings, 68 Me. 43 (1877); Brinson v. Mill Suply Co., 219 N.C. 498, 14 S.E.2d 505 (1941).

[5] Barry v. Merchants Exchange, 1 Samdf. Ch. 280 (1844); Lucas v. White Line Trans. Co., 70 Iowa, 541.

[6] Perrine v. Chesapeake & Delaware Canal Co., 9 How. 172 (1850); Bissell v. Michigan Southern & Northern Indiana R. Co., 22 N.Y. 258 (1860).

[7] Beach v. Fulton Bank, 3 Wend. 574 (1829); Hood v. New York and K.H.R. Co., 22 Conn. 502 (1853); Thomas v. Railroad Co., 101 U.S. 71 (1879); Central Transportation Co. v. Pullman Palace Car Co., 139 U.S. 24 (1890); Jacksonville M. P. Ry. Co., v. Hooper, 160 US 514, 16 S.Ct. 379 (1896); Joseph Schlitz Brewing Co. v. Missouri Poultry and Game Co., 287 Mo. 400, 229 S.W. 813 (1921); Texas Co. v. Z & M Independent Oil Co., 156 F2d 862 (1946). A comprehensive analytic review of the ultra vires doctrine from a case law perspective in the United States, in Colson (1936), pp. 206–217.

[8] Reese (1897) §30.

[9] It has become quite common in England in recent years to see the American term 'corporation' used instead of 'company'. Some universities have chairs of 'corporate' law. Courses on company law in American universities are usually called 'Corporations Law' and their legislation, state 'corporations' statutes. Over the years the word 'company' has been used in the UK instead of 'corporation' probably mainly for historical reasons. The early joint-stock companies used 'company' rather than 'corporation' and the word became part of the title of the statute, which was the foundation of

legal subject. For example, in civil law systems since the enactment of the French Commercial Code in 1807 hitherto, the majority of scholars across the world have shown a unique interest in all the areas of corporate law not only in their own legal systems but comparatively too.[10] This intellectual curiosity reached Anglo-Saxon jurists who had achieved notable progress in this science. Thus, for many legal writers the most notorious of the 19th century was the ultra vires doctrine in 1804[11]

---

modern company law, the Joint Stock Companies Act 1844. Since 1862 the statutes have been entitled 'Companies Act' and their provisions invariably refer to 'company' and 'companies'. Nearly all the textbooks speak of 'company law' and university courses are usually similarly titled. However, the Companies Act makes it clear that a company is a corporation, and, for example, CA 2006s. 16(2) provides that the effect of registration under the Act is that from the date of 'incorporation' the members of the company 'shall be a body corporate'.

The problem with using the word 'corporations' instead of companies in English law is that even today, 'corporations' is a broader concept than 'companies'. There are two main types of corporations: corporations 'sole' and corporations 'aggregate'. A corporation sole is an office or public appointment that is deemed to be independent of the human being who happens to fill the office from time to time. Originally, most corporations sole were ecclesiastical so that archbishops, bishops, canons, vicars, and so on were, and still are, corporations sole. Nevertheless, there are also many corporations soles, such as the sovereign, government ministers, and non-ministerial offices. A corporation sole will have the normal incidents of corporateness such as perpetual succession, so that when the individual occupying the office dies, the corporation sole, unchanged, is still there and can be filled by someone else. It is clear from all this that a company is not a corporation sole, hence, perhaps, the historical English law reluctance to use the word 'corporation' as a synonym for 'company', for while all companies are corporations, not all corporations are companies. Thus a company is a corporation aggregate, a corporation made up of a totality of individuals. Cf. Pettet (2012), p. 15.

In Australian corporate law, the terms "company" and "corporation" are often interchangeable, however, the Corporation Act 2001 regards a company, or its predecessor, registered under that Act as one class of corporation. A corporation also includes other artificial legal entities such as trade unions and incorporated associations as well as entities formed in other countries. See, Lipton (2008), 2. Regardless of historical or conceptual differentiation, in this writing, we will use both terms 'corporation' and 'company' as synonymous. It looks that this was the path followed by Armour (2017), 1. Nevertheless, comparative law authors point out that to avoid giving the impression that an entity having a separate legal personality is necessarily involved, these terms, i.e., corporation and company are thus often translated by the more general English expression "company", instead of by the word "corporation". Cf. Schlesinger (1998), pp. 887–888.

[10] Colfavru (1863), Streichenberger (1933), Gower (1956), Sternberg (1982), Tunc (1985), Santuari (1993), Foster (2000).

[11] Although foundations of the ultra vires doctrine may be found in the middle of the nineteenth century in equity courtesy of the leading cases of Coleman v. Eastern Counties Ry. Co. (1846), and in law of Eastern Anglian Ry. Co. v. Eastern Counties Ry. Co. (1851), however, long before this time it had been recognized in the United States as a corporate law doctrine, as early as 1804 in Head v. Providence; and subsequently in Buckley v. Derby (1817); People v. Utica (1818); Fireman Ins. Co. v. Sturgis (1824); Bank of United States v. Dandridge (1827); Beach v. Fulton Bank (1829); Bank of Augusta v. Earle (1839); Barry v. Merchants' Exchange (1844); Perrine v. Chesapeake (1850). Having been thus recognized and early rooted as a scion of corporate law, it has become an important doctrine relating both to private and municipal corporations, although the application of the ultra vires doctrine has been somewhat restrained and limited by the requirements of commercial law and the application of equitable principles in the dispensation of justice. See, Field (1881), pp. 579–580.

and its subsequent developments.[12] However, at the same time, it is right to claim that: "There is perhaps no part of the law concerning corporations in which we meet with so much difficulty, confusion, and conflict of opinion as in that which relates to the legal effect of ultra vires transactions".[13] Thus, for instance, French Professor Tunc held that the ultra vires doctrine in corporate law just matters in the cases of donations and other kinds of gratuitous acts involving the company's patrimony.[14]

According to Holdsworth,[15] in the Middle Ages, lawyers were beginning to deduce certain conclusions as to the powers, capacities, and liabilities of corporations from the nature of corporate personality. This process was pursued during this period; and consequently, certain rules were found as to activities from which the nature of that personality debarred corporations, and as to activities that were naturally incidental to corporate life. However, though it is possible to say that the nature of corporate personality debars corporations from some activities, it is difficult to draw the line in particular cases; and from that time forward, there has been a considerable fluctuation of opinion as to whether or not certain activities are permissible.

---

[12] Some classic commentators, however, have shown reluctance towards the ultra vires doctrine. For instance, Morawetz (1886), p. iv, stressed in the preface of his book: "The views of the author in respect to the proper treatment of the subject generally considered under the heading of 'Ultra Vires' have been confirmed by further reflection. The expression ultra vires has not been used in the text, partly because it is too vague to serve any useful purpose, and partly because the variety of significances attributed to it lead to inevitable confusion of thought".

Another criticism arises from business law practitioners because, in England and the USA, the ultra vires doctrine stood in the way of merger transactions. Until 1898 when New Jersey changed its law, corporations in the USA could not acquire shares in other corporations, as this was deemed to be beyond the purpose of typical manufacturing or trading corporations. From this perspective, the ultra vires doctrine became an obstacle to merger transactions that aimed to energize the economy.

[13] Ballantine (1930), p. 234. In fact, on behalf of the courts, the ultra vires was named an "indecent" doctrine. In re Norwich v. Norfolk. Indeed, the ultra vires doctrine has been frequently characterized as odious, ungracious, and unwelcome; and it is manifest that in its unqualified and rigid application, it frequently overrides the fundamental principles of equity; as for example, where the corporation is permitted to ignore an ultra vires contract, and at the same time retain the property or other consideration received under it. However, the original ultra vires doctrine it is gratifying to notice has been so molded and qualified by the courts that it has lost much of its frigid and austere character, and is, year after year, being limited in its application by the requirements of commercial law and the enforcement of the precepts of equity and the principles of common justice. Vid. Field (1881), p. 580.

[14] Tunc (1985), p. 44.

[15] Holdsworth (1922), pp. 385–386. It has been previously noticed by Blackstone, that the incidents which are tacitly annexed to every corporation as soon as it is duly erected are: (i) to have perpetual succession; (ii) to sue and be sued; (iii) to purchase lands; (iv) to have a common seal; and, (v) to make by-laws or private statutes for the better government of the corporation. The first three capacities are reducible to this, that the fictitious person of the corporation shall have, in general, the capacity of acting as an actual person, so far as the nature of the case admits. Such must have been the recognized law ever since corporations, as we understand the word, existed; for the conception of a corporation as a legal person, a conception going back farther than can be traced, involves necessarily the consequence that before the law the corporation shall be treated like any other person. See, Williston (1888), p. 117. The historical foundations of corporations and corporateness from a political and public law perspective, in Laski (1917) *passim*.

Similarly, it is complicated to determine what kind of activities are incident to corporate life; and, in the evolution of the law on this matter, the disturbing influence of semi-political considerations may be suspect. Most corporations at this period were created by royal charter; and, to allow a royal charter to vary the incidents attached by common law to corporate capacities appeared to contravene the principle that a royal charter cannot change the law. Hence there was a tendency to define corporate powers and capacities somewhat rigidly and to deny that the crown could limit the powers incident to a corporation. Nevertheless, it was desirable to maintain some measure of control over corporate activities. This fact was recognized by law; and it soon became apparent that, as the purposes for which corporations were formed were varied, it was hard to hold that all corporations created by royal charter must have the same powers and capacities.

Hence, in addition to older modes of controlling corporate activities, the inception of a restriction on these activities is based on the purposes for which a corporation has created a limitation which, in later law, will assume enormous importance. Though it may not be within the competence of the crown to change the incidents annexed by law to corporate personality, it is within the power of the crown to define the purposes for which a corporation is created; and if the corporation tries to effect purposes other than those for which it was created, its acts will be ultra vires and void.

On the other hand, in the United Kingdon, it was not until the latter part of the 19th century that the strict type of ultra vires was applied to companies. Until 1844 the most common class of company had no corporate personality; that was enjoined only by chartered companies and by companies directly incorporated by statute. After the Joint Stock Companies Act 1856, the deed of settled companies became superseded by registered incorporated companies with limited liability and a memorandum of association that had to specify their objects. Only then were the courts forced to decide whether the ultra vires doctrine applied.[16] The 'company' under the 1844 Act was still a partnership on which certain corporate attributes had been conferred. It was not subject to the ultra vires doctrine. However, the intention of the legislature from 1856 onwards was for capacity to be defined by the simple specification of an object which could not be changed.[17]

The first reported case touching on the application of the ultra vires doctrine in England was *Colman v. Eastern Counties Ry. Co. 10 Beau. 1 (1846)*, where the

[16] Gower (2003), p. 132. Until 1844 companies scarcely existed and did so because either a monarch had granted a charter of incorporation, as with the Honorable East India Co., or because Parliament granted a charter of incorporation, as the Scots Parliament did on the incorporation of the Bank of Scotland in 1695. Vid. Grier (2005), pp. 1–2.

[17] Farrar (1998), p. 98. In the opinion of this author, the ultra vires doctrine does not apply to chartered corporations. At common law chartered corporations seem to have been regarded as having all the powers of a natural person in spite of the practice of specifying express objects in the charter. From Coke onwards, this seems to have been regarded as the law. In re Sutton Hospital (1612) 10 Co Rep 1a, 23a. This does not mean, however, that a chartered corporation can never be stopped from acting outside its charter. In *Institution of Mechanical Engineers* v. *Cane*, Lord Denning in the House of Lords thought that anyone injured thereby could apply for an injunction to prevent a chartered corporation acting outside its objects. See, Farrar (1998), p. 99.

question arose on a motion to dissolve a special injunction. In this case, as Pollock observed, the House of Lords decided that, as regards companies established under the general provisions of the Companies Act of 1862, the memorandum of association (a public and registered document specifying the company's objects) is a fundamental constitution or "unalterable law" which the company has no power to enlarge. The directors of a railway company, to increase the traffic, proposed to guaranty certain profits and to secure the capital of an intended steam packet company, which were to act in connection with the railway. It was held that such a transaction was not within their powers, and they were restrained and the injunction made perpetual.[18]

The case, however, most frequently quoted, and the one wherein the ultra vires doctrine is most exhaustively considered, discussed and the question finally settled in England, came before the House of Lords on appeal from the Court of Exchequer in 1875, as *Ashbury Ry. Co. v. Riche, 7 H. L. 653 (1875).* A company was registered under the Joint Stock Companies Act of 1862. Its objects, as declared in the memorandum of association, were:

> To make and sell, or lend on hire, railway carriages and wagons, and all kinds of railway plant, fittings, machinery and rolling-stock; to carry on the business of mechanical engineers and *general contractors*; to purchase, work, lease and sell mines, minerals, land and buildings; to purchase and sell, as merchants, timber, coal, metals or other materials, and to buy and sell any such materials on commission or as agents. (italics supplied)

The directors agreed to purchase a concession for making a railway in a foreign country and afterward agreed to consign the concession to a *societé anonyme* formed in that country, which *societé* was to supply the materials for the construction of the railway, and to receive periodical payments from the English company. It was held that this contract, being of nature not included in the memorandum of association, was ultra vires not only of the directors but also of the company, so that even the subsequent assent of the whole body of shareholders would have no power to ratify it.[19]

From a detailed analysis of historical case law involving ultra vires issues, it is possible to conclude that a corporation is commonly styled a "legal person", but the appellation "person" applies to it only by analogy; and the analogy fails when it is thus clearly stated that this legal person is wanting in much that belongs to a natural person—that its course of existence is marked out from its birth; that it has been called into being for certain special purposes; that it has all the powers and capacities, and only those, which are expressly given it or are requisite for the due

---

[18] Reese (1897) §39. The origins of the ultra vires doctrine, as applicable to companies registered under the Companies Acts, however, can be traced back to 1843 when Bellenden Ker, as a witness before the Select Committee on Joint Stock Companies, suggested as a measure against stock-jobbing: 'There should be a provision preventing altering the nature of the undertaking (to be precisely described in the deed), except on having a new deed'. See, Horrwitz (1946), p. 66.

[19] Reese (1897) §41. The doctrine taught in *Ashbury* was subsequently followed in Attorney-General v. Great Eastern Ry. Co., 5 App. Cas. 473 (1880); Small et al. v. Smith et al. 10 App. Cas. 119 (1884); Baroness Wenlock, etc. v. The Ewer Dee, 10 App. Cas. 354 (1885); Trevor et al. v. Whitworth et al. 12 App. Cas. 409 (1887).

carrying out of those purposes; and that all the obligations it affects to assume which do not arise from or out of the pursuit of such purposes, are null and void.[20]

2.2 The Ultra Vires Doctrine in Corporate Law

Prior to teaching the main features of the ultra vires doctrine in corporate law, it is expedient to make a brief approach to the Roman concept of "personality" in private law, taking into account the research of Duff.[21] It seems that, whatever the case may have been under the Republic, it was laid down in 7 B.C. by the *lex lulia de Collegiis* that every college which received permission to exist was automatically endowed with all the rights and duties which were conveyed to these writers' minds by the phrases 'Privatrechts und Handlungsfähigkeit', and 'personnaliti civile, morale', or 'juridique'; except that there might have been some restrictions in respect of immovables, and that, for fear of powerful corporations or of the Dead Hand, the rights of *testamenti factio and* manumission were arbitrarily denied. Waltzing said in 1896 that once provided with this authorization (of the Emperor or the Senate) and recognized by the state, the college becomes a public institution, a public body (*corpus*). However, any public body receives with existence civil personification. So Saleilles, in a lecture delivered in 1907, stated that an association was lawful only by authorization; but, as soon as it was lawful, it was capable, it had civil personality. It was all or nothing. The idea of the 'corps public' has been dealt with already under the guise of 'utiliti positive'. There is no evidence for interference by the State in the affairs of colleges, except to control their birth, in or before the classical law; and to call a burial club of the Roman type a 'corps public' is an abuse of language. But in concern with the other part of the belief the view that every authorized college was given 'personnalité civile' by the *lex Julia.*[22]

According to the legislation of every country, human beings have the rights and capacity to bind themselves in a variety of manners utilizing contracts. Conversely, due to the lack of a corporeal entity, the powers, and capacities, the rights and liabilities of the firms to interact in the business environment, are limited by legal provisions strictly to carry out only those purposes for whom they have been established and through those persons appointed as directors; consequently, corporations can only act within their chartered powers. The majority of scholars agree that a key attribute of corporations is to have a legal personality as a juristic person; however, there are some theoretical discussions as to its exact legal nature. We must recognize that a firm can simply enter into the business world through a legal entity regardless of

[20] Brice (1893), p. 40.

[21] Duff (1971), pp. 137–138.

[22] Duff (1971), pp. 137–138.

the attributes of its directors and stockholders. In this respect, there is a distinction between corporate authority and the capacity of its directors.[23]

Some criticism, however, arises about this assertion because the formula that a corporation has no "*powers*" expect such as are conferred by its charter cannot and does not mean that it has no "*capacity*" to acquire rights and liabilities by the ultra vires acts of its representatives. A corporation has no *authority* to do acts which are not within the scope of its business, but, as in the case of an individual, the law may find ground to ascribe to it a legal responsibility for acts done by its agents, though not strictly authorized. They may exceed its proper corporate purposes and do an ultra vires act, and the act will be, in contemplation of the law, not merely the act of the officers or stockholders, but the act of the corporation itself.[24]

The distinction between a natural person and one of statutory creation may be said to be this: natural persons are not confined in the exercise of their capacities to any particular act or business but may do any act or enter into any contract not prohibited by law. An artificial person may do no acts nor enter into any contract except such as are authorized by law; the one's powers being inherent while the powers of the other are conferred.[25] Therefore, when a firm exceeds those legal provisions or articles of association, the ultra vires doctrine arises.

The ultra vires doctrine in corporate law has been studied over many decades and from different approaches. The analysis extends from business transactions to philanthropic acts.[26] Thus, it is correct to point out that this is not a newcomer in

---

[23] A long time ago in England, the Courts held that Royal charter corporations have the capacity of natural persons and their contracts though ultra vires were valid. In re British South Africa Co. v. De Beers (1910) I Ch. 354, 375. Carpenter (1923), p. 50. A detailed analysis of the linguistic basis of treating the corporation as a person, in Schane (1986) *passim*. As this author notes corporations are never *people*, but they can be *persons*. It is an interesting lexical curiosity that "people" as one of the plural forms of "person" refers uniquely to real persons. On the other hand, scholars also have dealt with constitutional issues arising from corporate personality, both rights, and obligations, Vid. Note (1982) *passim*.

[24] Ballantine (1930), p. 242.

[25] Reese (1897) §5. An insight about this issue, by Dewby (1926), p. 658, who claims that the postulate, which has been a controlling principle although usually made unconsciously, leading to the merging of popular and philosophical notions of the person with the legal notion, is the conception that before anything can be a jural person it must intrinsically possess certain properties, the existence of which is necessary to constitute anything a person. Taking into account the previous statement, from our point of view it is not correct to argue that: "Even though a company is an artificial entity, it has the *same* legal capacity and powers as a human being. It is, therefore, able to engage in any business or activity and may acquire and exercise rights in the same way as an individual" (italics supplied). Vid. Lipton (2008), p. 2.

Let us just mention the elemental argument to be advised about the distinction: corporations cannot get married and natural persons cannot issue shares. A moderate vision is exposed by Hanrahan (2008), 22–140, who claims that when a new company is created by registration, the Corporation Act 2001 confers on that company power to do acts that have legal effect. In many respects, the capacity of a company to do acts having legal effects is the same as that of a natural person.

[26] In the nineteenth century, judges often treated corporate actions such as charitable contributions and expenditures on behalf of employees as beyond the power of the corporation, or ultra vires. Under modern corporate law, such actions are routinely upheld. Thus, charitable contributions may

the commercial law landscape, but probably this legal mechanism could be the most critically acclaimed to some scholars, and at the same time, controversial[27] because it has to deal with a cardinal principle grounded in a market economy system: the freedom of enterprise[28]; and likewise a pendulum movement, the research interest has come and gone chiefly motivated to some judicial decisions and lately legislation enacted about it.

As we have seen previously, few subjects have elicited more discussion or excited more general interest in the law of corporations than the ultra vires doctrine. Reese

---

create favorable publicity for the firm and be an effective form of advertising. Contributions then are like perquisites, which courts also decline to investigate leaving such questions to markets, demonstrating conformity of law and economics. See, Easterbrook (1996), p. 102.

In *AP Smith Manufacturing Co v Barlow*, 13 N.J. 145, 98 A. 2d 581 (N.J. 1953) the Court held that a donation made by a company to a university is not ultra vires:

> There is no hesitancy in sustaining the validity of the donation. There is no suggestion that it was made indiscriminately or to a pet charity of the corporate directors in furtherance of personal rather than corporate ends. Conversely, it was made to a preeminent institution [Princeton University] was modest in amount [$1.500] and well within the limitations imposed by the statutory enactments, and was voluntarily made in the reasonable belief that it would aid the public welfare and advance the interests of the plaintiff as a private corporation and as part of the community in which it operates. It was a lawful exercise of the corporation's implied and incidental powers under common-law principles and that it came within the express authority of the pertinent state legislation.

[27] In this case, the court remarked that "... modern conditions require that corporations acknowledge and discharge social as well as private responsibilities as a member of the community within which they operate". In the opinion of Clark (1986), p. 682, note 11, this language seems unnecessary to the holding, given the court's espousal of the theory that the gift in question was for the corporation's indirect benefit, and it is unclear that the court intended anything more than to express a rationale for traditional corporate giving, which was sanctioned by statute in New Jersey, where the corporation was domiciled and the donee organization located.

A thoughtful analysis about this topic in Harriman (1954), Eisenberg (1998), Klein (2003), pp. 270–286. In re Lee, Behrens & Co Ltd. [1932] 2 Ch. 46, UK courts postulated the following test for the validity of corporate gifts: (i) Is the transaction reasonably incidental to the carrying on of the company's business? (ii) Is it a *bona fide* transaction? and (iii) Is it done for the benefit of and to promote the prosperity of the company? This test was applied in *Parke v. Daily News Ltd.* and *W & M Roith Ltd.*, but subsequently rejected in *Charterbridge Ltd. v. Lloyds Bank* and *Horsley & Weight Ltd.*

There were two legislative developments germane to the decline of the ultra vires doctrine. Firstly, restrictions on the numbers and types of purposes for which a business could be incorporated disappeared. Secondly, the amendment of the purpose clause by corporate action was expressly authorized. The emergence of these enabling acts presaged the eventual demise of the concession theory. See, Schaeftler (1983), p. 89.

[28] Cf. Berle (1948) claiming that early corporations did have a grant of limited powers dictated by a definite public policy. The state feared that corporations would grow to anti-social size; or would monopolize economic life by engaging in many activities. Thus, the limitation of powers was an attempt to impose social control on the new form of business organization. The conception was that limitation and control could be achieved by making corporate action impossible beyond the field of activity marked out for it by the state.

states that the term ultra vires is the modern legal nomenclature for acts of a corporation that exceed or are beyond the powers conferred by law upon the legal entity, acting through any of its instrumentalities.[29] The expression ultra vires is used in different senses, to express that the act of the directors oversteps their authority as agents of the corporation, or that the act of the majority of the stockholders is in violation of the rights of the minority, or that the act has not been done in conformity with the requirements of the charter, or the act is one which the corporation itself has not the capacity to do, as being in excess of the corporate powers.[30]

The ultra vires doctrine was envisioned in its very first stage to protect the shareholders from the abuses of the company's directors; and secondly, to protect the creditors' pecuniary rights.[31] Shareholders are the company's owners, however, the commercial reality has shown that not all of them are capable to enforce their rights in a proper, timely, and effective manner, in particular, those with monetary content. Therefore, they have an action at law in pursuit of protection for such wrongdoing.

On the other hand, at its original conception, the ultra vires doctrine aimed to protect the creditors' rights against behaviors committed by directors beyond their powers through unauthorized commercial activities and even gratuitous acts such as philanthropic gifts.[32] Some criticisms arose about this point because the entrepreneurs ought to have perfect information about economic transactions in which they are involved. Moreover, for instance, when a bank lends money is its duty to make sure that the debtor will repay it. In this way, regardless of the investments or expenditures made by the borrower or whether these have a direct connection with the firm's objects clause, the lender has a guaranty to get his money back.[33]

---

[29] Reese (1897) §17.

[30] See footnote 29.

[31] According to Carpenter (1923), p. 65, the violation of the interests of creditors can hardly be urged as a sufficient ground upon which to rest the ultra vires doctrine. It is probably the law that the creditor has no right to complain of an ultra vires transaction unless his security is endangered. This is a right that should exist independently of any ultra vires doctrine. It would hardly seem justifiable to establish for the benefit of creditors a doctrine which would result in annulling a contract deliberately entered into when the creditor's interest is considered insufficient to entitle them to direct relief. In fact, the courts have not seriously treated the creditor's interest as requiring the ultra vires doctrine for its proper protection.

[32] In *Anglo Overseas Agencies Ltd. v. Green*, it was suggested that where creditors had entered into a contract with a company that was ultra vires, they could escape liability, even if they caused the company damage, see Baxt (1971), p. 306. From our point of view, however, this thesis must be discarded, inasmuch as businessmen ought to have complete information about the director's powers. To allow this situation could trigger perverse incentives in the application of the ancient roman aphorism: "*nemo auditur propriam turpitudinem allegans*".

[33] (1875) L.R. 7 H.L. 653. Applied in Ireland *Balgooley Distillery* (1886) 17 L.R. Ir. 239 and *Cummins, Barton v Bank of Ireland* [1939] I.R. 60. In the latter case, the bank knowingly lent money to a company for a purpose ultra vires the powers of the company. The Court held that the bank was not entitled, on the voluntary liquidation of the company, to be admitted as a creditor of the company in respect of the money so lent. Both cases made specific use of the *Ashbury* authority, at 672-3 of that judgment, that if a transaction is void on the ground of ultra vires, it is void ab initio; therefore, the shareholders cannot subsequently ratify it. See also *Hennessy v National Agricultural*

It is important to take into account that an ultra vires act or transaction does not necessarily imply an illegal behavior committed by the directors; it is all about acting beyond the corporate's capacity. On this basis, all of the illegal activities must be treated outside this doctrine and the compensation prosecuted through another kind of legal tool.

Carpenter claims that corporations are impliedly prohibited by statute from making contracts beyond their authorized powers.[34] Accordingly, ultra vires contracts must then in one sense be considered illegal. Nevertheless, should the ultra vires contract be treated as an ordinary illegal contract? The nature of the objection to the ultra vires contract differs fundamentally from the nature of the objection to the illegal contract. The objection to the illegal contract as distinguished from the ultra vires contract relates to the subject matter. The objection to the ultra vires contract relates to the capacity of the corporation to do such acts, to the fact that the corporation is going beyond the authority given it in the articles of incorporation. There is nothing inimical to social welfare in ultra vires activity in itself. Illegality will not explain the law of ultra vires. It will not do than to rest ultra vires upon illegality. To do so is unsound theoretically and gives us results that are not only incompatible with the decisions but also undesirable because unfair.[35]

We cast doubts about this theory because an act committed beyond the powers (ultra vires) of the company is *illegal* in itself. Indeed, it makes no sense to separate two conducts prohibited by law and count them against the law twice. We do not adhere to the idea that the chief difference between an "ordinary illegal contract" and another one under the ultra vires umbrella deals with the lack of capacity going beyond the authority given in the articles of incorporation. Just suppose that a firm—ABC—runs a business without a mandatory special license and one of its providers would like to file a suit against it for a breach of contract. In this hypothesis, ABC does not have the capacity for running the business because it has not met the legal requirements. On the other hand, in the articles of incorporation of the company XYZ, it was pointed out that the directors may only lease a property for headquarters up to $1.000 monthly, but the directors make an agreement for $2.000. There is also a legal violation in this second case, insofar as this agreement is against the articles of incorporation because it has been done beyond the powers of incorporation.

In turn, Berle has pointed out the unjustified use of the phrase in connection with illegal conduct where the corporation has full power to do the act, but to do it must proceed in a prescribed manner.[36] For example, when a firm has the power to increase

---

and Industrial Development Association [1947] I.R. 159 at 203. Vid. Anderson (2003), p. 263, footnote 29.

[34] Carpenter (1923), pp. 60–61.

[35] See footnote 34.

[36] Berle (1948), p. 45.

its capital stock upon the board of directors authorizing an appropriate vote by the shareholders at a meeting specially called for the purpose. If the increase of stock was authorized by a minority of the board, the resulting stock issue is sometimes loosely said to have been "ultra vires" but the term is misused.[37]

Up to this point, we have approached the ultra vires doctrine in corporate law in connection with the corporate personality and capacity, and some criticisms regarding its legal nature and usefulness in everyday business life. Subsequently, we will study the doctrine from three different angles in accordance with the main juristic families: (i) common law (USA, UK, and Australia); European civil law (French, Germany, Italy, and Spain); and, (iii) Latin America (Argentina, Brasil, Chile, Colombia, México, and Perú). We have chosen these jurisdictions, taking into account that the vast majority of countries around the world feed their legislature and case law from these juristic sources.[38]

---

[37] See footnote 36.

[38] As noted by Schlesinger (1998), pp. 896–898, the needs served and the functions performed by the modern business corporation are essentially the same in all highly industrialized countries which have preserved a measure of free enterprise, whether they belong to the civil-law or the common-law orbit. In spite of this fact, and in spite of the complexity of the historical cross-currents which have shaped the pertinent rules of law, it is still possible to observe, even in the area of corporation law, the impact of the methodological, procedural, and classificatory differences which generally exist between common law and civil law. For example: (a) the absence in civil law of separate equity courts and of their flexible procedures; (b) two institutions which in the civil-law form are unknown to the common-law systems: the notary and the commercial register; (c) the effect of the civilian dichotomy between civil and commercial law.

2.3 Should the Ultra Vires Doctrine Be Discarded at All?

Despite Carpenter asked whether the ultra vires doctrine should be *discarded*,[39] and others have held a thanatology view about its *death*[40] or that it is just a historical *curiosity*,[41] and even proclaiming it as *useless*,[42] the doctrine indeed applies in

[39] Carpenter (1923), p. 49. This author also asks: Should the ultra vires doctrine not be entirely discarded? Has it not made for complexity and confusion in the law? Is there any sound basis for it, any excuse for its existence? And will its abandonment not leave the law in a more satisfactory state? Throughout this writing, we will evidence how these questions are answered both positively and negatively. The life, death, and rebirth of the ultra vires doctrine in corporate law has rolled worldwide in the printing houses for more than two hundred years like a wandering ghost. In fact, this monograph allows evidencing it.

[40] Wedderburn (1966), pp. 673–676. The decision of *Bell Houses Ltd. v. City Wall Properties Ltd.* was reversed by the Court of Appeals. It will be recalled that the plaintiff, a property company which, in the person of its chairman, had used its knowledge of sources of finance to secure for the defendants "bridging finance" of about £1 million, brought an action to recover commission allegedly due to it on the transaction. The defendants pleaded that this contract to act as a money broker was ultra vires to the plaintiff company. The Court thought that the contract was intra vires and left open the "interesting, important and difficult question" whether the defendants could have taken the point had it been ultra vires. In this respect, according to Wedderburn, with a well-drafted clause in subjective terms no company needs to be bothered by it again. It will have the capacity to do any act which its directors decide to do. In all this, the Court showed the strongest disinclination to allow the ultra vires principle any scope, especially in transactions with outsiders. Lastly, Wedderburn concludes that the victory of the subjective objects clause must be the beginning of the end of the ultra vires doctrine.

In the same argumentative context, Baxt (1971), p. 301, casts doubts about the survival of the doctrine, and laconically claims: "... most traditions die hard and it seems that, despite a long apparently successful defense campaign, the supporters of the ultra vires doctrine would now admit that if it is not dead it is no more than a walking corpse". In fact, since 1894, William Cook, a prominent corporation's treatise writer, noted that the traditional ultra vires doctrine was disappearing rapidly. By 1898, he proclaimed it dead, at least in state courts. Fundamental to this development was the prevailing use of general incorporation acts rather than special charters. Some state courts held that the powers of a corporation formed under a general statute should be construed more broadly than those of a corporation created by special charter because the former was more like an ordinary person engaged in business. See, Hovenkamp (1988), pp. 1663–1664.

[41] Palmiter (1991), p. 454. In the words of such author, the modem corporate law appears as a state-provided service that offers those seeking to structure their business relationship a relatively standardized, off-the-rack package consisting of a governance structure, legal personality, delineation of ownership rights, and limited liability for the corporate participants. The package is roughly analogous to a state-written form partnership agreement, with state-provided immunity from participant liability. Only a small set of rules remains mandatory, and their scope is diminishing: the ultra vires has become a historical curiosity. On the other hand, Berle (1948), p. 46, stresses that when a true question of ultra vires is raised under a modern charter, it is generally proof of poor draftsmanship on the part of the incorporating lawyers. There may have practical importance when dealing with an ancient charter or a badly drafted certificated of incorporation.

[42] Schaeftler (1983), p. 81. This author points out ab initio of his Article that frequently a landmark decision, major statutory modification, or new phenomenon occurring in a changing society generates scholarly debate over a legal doctrine. Obsession with a legal doctrine often fades following the legislative adoption of a workable solution illuminated previously in the professional literature and committee reports. That was the fate of the ultra vires doctrine in the USA.

some commercial activities and corporate law areas such as takeover scenarios,[43] and notwithstanding the many strong reasons for its downfall, it did not erode to nothingness. Rather, as Greenfield notes, an important part of it was retained and survives today. This vestige of the doctrine sets off illegal activities as ultra vires for corporations.[44] However, we will see how, with limited exceptions, in civil law jurisdictions across South America and Europe, nowadays the ultra vires doctrine in corporate law has plenty of validity.

Finally, some criticism about the ultra vires doctrine is its lack of practical application, bearing in mind that anomalies that arose from the excess of power can be resolved through a legal mechanism in accordance with the specific business transaction involved in it. Thus, for instance, when there is a legal issue concerning contracts or negotiable instruments, the rules affecting each one of those subject matters come into effect making the use of an estrange doctrine unnecessary. However, things are not as simple as that since not all cases can be resolved based on the particular rules of every kind of irregularity.

References

Anderson J (2003) Evolution of the ultra vires rule in Irish company law. Irish Jurist 38
Armour J et al (2017) The anatomy of corporate law, Oxford
Ballantine H (1930) Manual of Corporations law, Chicago
Baxt (1971) Is the doctrine of ultra vires dead? Int Comparative L Q 20(2)
Berle A et al (1948) Business Organizations, Brooklyn
Brice S (18930 A treatise on the doctrine of ultra vires, London
Carpenter C (1923) Should the doctrine of ultra vires be discarded? Yale L J 33(1)
Clark R (1986) Corporate law, New York
Colfavru J (1863) Droit Commercial Comparé de la France et de l'Angleterre, Paris
Colson C (1936) The doctrine of ultra vires in the united states supreme court decisions. W Va L Q 42:179
Dewby J (1926) Historic background of corporate legal personality. Yale L J 35
Duff P (1971) Personality in roman private law, New York
Easterbrook F et al (1996) Economic structure of corporate law, Cambridge
Eisenberg M (1998) Corporate conduct that does not maximize shareholder gain. Stetson L Rev 28(1)
Farrar J et al (1998) Company law, London
Field G (1881) The doctrine of ultra vires, Des Moines
Foster N (2000) Company law in comparative perspective: England and France. Am J Comparative L 48(4)
Gower L et al (2003) Principles of modern company law, London

[43] Kulwicki (1988), p. 848, argues that the ultra vires doctrine, unlike the business judgment rule, is designed to protect shareholder interests; therefore, the common law rule of construction is even better suited to the ultra vires doctrine in the takeover setting. Using the strict rule of construction, a shareholder's challenge to the board's adoption of an antitakeover device which creates a potential conflict of interest should be upheld if the plain words or necessary implication of the state's business corporation law does not support the board's authority to so act.

[44] Greenfield (2001), p. 1314.

Gower L (1956) Some contrasts between British and American corporation law. Harvard L Rev 69
Greenfield G (2001) Ultra vires lives! Virginia L Rev 87(7)
Grier N (2005) Company law, Edinburgh
Hanrahan P (2008) Commercial applications of company law, Sydney
Harriman D (1954) Corporations: donations to private education. California L Rev 4:41
Holdsworth (1922) History of English law, Boston
Horrwitz W (1946) Company law reform and ultra vires doctrine. L Q Rev 62:66
Hovenkamp H (1988) The classical corporation in American legal thought. Georgetown L J 76
Klein W et al (2003) Business Associations, New York
Kulwicki D (1988) Auspicious return of the ultra vires doctrine. Ohio State L J 49(3)
Laski H (1917) The early history of the corporation in England. Harvard L Rev 30
Lipton P (2008) Understanding company law, Sydney
Morawetz V (1886) Treatise on the law of private corporations, Boston
Note (1982) Constitutional rights of the corporate person. Yale L J 91:1641
Palmiter A (1991) Stanching the federalization of corporate law. Wash U L Q 69:445
Pettet B (2012) Company law, Harlow
Reese R (1897) The doctrine of ultra vires, Chicago
Santuari A (1993) The joint stock company in nineteenth century: England and France. J Leg Hist 14:39
Schaeftler M (1983) Ultra vires—ultra useless. J Corp L 9:81
Schane S (1986) Corporation is a person: the language of a legal fiction. Tulane L Rev 61:563
Schlesinger R et al (1998) Comparative law, New York
Sternberg M (1982) The close corporation's counterparts in France, Germany, and the United Kingdom. Hastings Int Comparative L Rev 5:291
Streichenberger J (1933) Societés Anonymes de France et d'Angleterre, Paris
Swaney H (1883) Essay on ultra vires, Washington
Tunc A (1985) Droit Américain des Sociétés Anonymes, Paris
Wedderburn (1966) The death of ultra vires? Modern L Rev 29
Williston S (1888) History of the law of business corporations before 1800. Harvard L Rev 3

Chapter 3
The Ultra Vires Doctrine in Common Law

Abstract In this chapter, an analysis of the ultra vires doctrine in common law is provided. We address from ancient until modern adjudications and legislation, taking into account that the roots of such a doctrine may be found both in the United States and latterly in the United Kingdom case law. Finally, there will be a study of the Australian jurisdiction because of recent legislative developments.

Over the last century, common law has had a remarkable influence in Roman-German legal tradition families worldwide, due greatly to its pragmatism and solidity. Vitality and tenacity are not new qualities in common law tradition. It has been able to receive the most diverse doctrines and rules developed outside of it, without disturbing its essential unity. Furthermore, in that legal system, it is possible to forecast with some certainty the upcoming court's adjudications. The growth of such a custom depends to some extent on the habit of following precedents, although it is more than likely that this development took place quite unconsciously. From the earliest times, courts have had some sort of regard for previous decisions.[1] On this groundwork and bearing in mind that the ultra vires doctrine is a creature born and raised in a common law system, we are going to commence exploring it there.

3.1 United States

Since the very first appearance of the ultra vires doctrine in common law, the most important field of application has been contract law, and concretely, as a juristic mechanism of defense. It must be noted that a distinction is made between contracts which are: (a) unauthorized because not granted expressly or by implication; (b) merely an irregular exercise of a granted power; (c) intrinsically immoral or against

[1] Holdsworth (1922), pp. 194, et seq., Pound (1931), pp. 4–5, Holmes (1923), pp. 1–2; Plucknett (1956), p. 342.

M. A. Jiménez Sánchez, *The Ultra Vires Doctrine in Corporate Law*,
SpringerBriefs in Law, https://doi.org/10.1007/978-3-030-88838-1_3

public policy, *malum in se*; and, (d) prohibited by the charter or general law, *malum prohibitum*.[2]

In turn, ultra vires contracts may be classified, for the purpose of determining their effect in: (1) contracts executed on both sides, which the courts will not set aside or interfere with for the purpose of depriving either party of what has been acquired under them; (2) contracts executory on both sides, which will not be enforced at the suit of either party; (3) contracts executed on one side, and executory on the other, which the courts in some jurisdictions, will enforce in favor of the party that has executed the same for its part against the other party that has received and retains the benefits; (4) contracts, whether wholly executory or executed on one side, apparently authorized, but in fact ultra vires because made for a purpose, not within the scope of the corporation's business, or made without observing prescribed formalities, the ultra vires purpose, or the failure to observe the prescribed formalities, being unknown to the other party, which contracts are enforceable against the corporation; (5) contracts evidenced by a negotiable instrument, which is valid and binding upon the corporation in the hands of a *bona fide* purchaser, the instrument being apparently within the powers of the corporation, but having been given for an ultra vires purpose, or in an ultra vires transaction; (6) contracts which are not only ultra vires, but also illegal, because in violation of an express statutory prohibition or contrary to public policy, such contracts being void because of their illegality, aside from the fact that they are also ultra vires, on the same principles which render illegal contracts between individuals void.[3]

A contract by which a corporation disables itself from performing its functions and duties undertaken and imposed by its charter is, unless the state which created it consents, ultra vires. A charter not only grants rights; it also imposes duties. Acceptance of those rights is an assumption of those duties. As it is a contract that binds the state not to interfere with those rights, so, likewise, it is one that binds the corporation to carry out the discharge of those duties. It is not like a deed or patent, which vests in the grantee or patentee not only the title but the full power of alienation, but it is more, it is a contract whose obligations neither party, state nor corporation, can, without the consent of the other, abandon.[4]

> There are few rules better settled or more strongly supported by authority, with fewer exceptions in this country, than that when a contract by a private corporation, which is otherwise unobjectionable, has been performed on one side, the party which has received and retains the benefit of such performance shall not be permitted to evade performance on the ground that the contract was in excess of the purpose for which the company was created. The rule may not be strictly logical, but it prevents a great deal of injustice.[5]

In the pioneer case *Ashbury*, Lord Cairns taught: "I have used the expressions *extra vires* and *intra vires*. I prefer either expression very much to one which occasionally has been used. In other cases, the expression 'illegality' ... In a case such as that

---

[2] Elliott (1911) §200.

[3] Ballantine (1930), p. 251.

[4] R. L & P. R. Co. *v.* Union Pac. Ry. Co., 47 Fed. Rep. 15.

[5] Seymour v. Chicago Guaranty, etc., Soc., 54 Minn. 147, 55 N. W. 907.

which your Lordships have now to deal with, it is not a question whether the contract sued upon involves that which is *malum prohibitum* or *malum in se*, or is a contract contrary to public policy, and illegal in itself ... The question is not as to the legality of the contract; the question is as to the competency and power of the company to make the contract".[6]

Another practical subject matter with respect to the ultra vires doctrine is the negotiable instruments law. Indeed, negotiable instruments are a key transactional mechanism in business life and they are typically issued for different purposes, such as a payment system (e.g., cheques), to get credit to finance commercial activities (e.g., promissory notes),[7] to mobilize goods (e.g., bills of lading), and to represent corporate rights (e.g., stocks). Historically, it has been held that corporate bodies may issue promissory notes and drafts where the nature and character of their business warrant it. Here the nature and character of the business are such that the issuing negotiable instruments would be an ordinary and almost necessary incident to it.[8]

The power to incur debts does not involve or imply the power to issue negotiable instruments in payment or on account of the same. "It is said that the company must necessarily incur debts in the prosecution of the business of carriers, but it is one thing to say that they shall be liable to be sued for goods sold and delivered or for work done, and an entirely different thing to say that they may accept bills in payment".[9] From our point of view, the American's ruling is more reasonable:

> No question is better settled upon authority than that a corporation, not prohibited by law from doing so, and without any express power in its charter for that purpose, may make a

[6] Ashbury Railway Carriage and Iron Co Ltd v Riche (1875) LR 7 HL 653.

[7] The maker of a note cannot object that a corporate holder purchased the note ultra vires. In re Prescott Nat'l Bank v. Butler, 157 Mass. 548, 32 N. E. 909 (1893). Neither can the obligor of a non-negotiable choice in action defend on the ground that the plaintiff corporation's purchase was ultra vires. In re John Farwell Co. v. Wolf, 96 Wis. 10, 70 N. W. 289 (1897). *Contra*: Pueblo v. Shutt Co., 28 Colo. 524, 67 Pac. 162 (1901). Cf. Stevens (1927), p. 306, footnote 37.

[8] Brice (1893), p. 247. In *New York Firemen, Ins. Co. v. Siurges*, 2 Cow. 664 (1824) someone of the leading cases in connection with the ultra vires doctrine involving negotiable instruments, was assumpsit against second indorsers on a promissory note, defendant company being one of the indorsers. In affirming the principle that corporations have no powers except such as are specially granted and those necessary to effect the powers so granted, it was held that a corporation has no power by the act of incorporation to discount notes, but created for the purpose of insurance, has no right to carry on the business of discounting. See, Reese (1897) §23. A bank that has accepted drafts to the plaintiff for value cannot set up the defense of ultra vires when sued on its indorsement even if the transaction is not strictly within the bank's powers. In re Sherrill vs. American Trust Co. 176 N.C. 591, 97 S.E. 471. Vid. Brannan (1926), p. 181.

[9] See, Keating, J. L. K. 1 C. P. 511. Cit., Brice (1893), p. 251. We do adhere to this author about the main question relating to ultra vires doctrine and negotiable instruments being: when is a corporation liable with respect to negotiable instruments? The answer is only when it has the power to issue or negotiate them. The liability depends purely on the question of power, as such in the strictest sense, and not upon any question of the purposes for which the documents were issued or to which their proceeds are applied. However, it has been said that the latter is the real point, op. cit., p. 263.

> negotiable promissory note, payable either at a future day or upon demand when such note is given for any of the legitimate purposes for which the company was incorporated.[10]

It is an acknowledged rule in the USA that the right to contract debts carries with it the power to give negotiable notes or bills in payment or security for such debts unless the corporations are in a like manner prohibited. It may therefore be established as a general rule, that a corporation not prohibited by law from so doing, and without any express power in its charter for that purpose, may make a negotiable promissory note, payable either at a future day or on-demand when such note is given for any of the legitimate purposes for which the company was incorporated.[11] However, as a general rule, an unauthorized signature binds no one and is entirely ineffective. In accordance with the UCC §3-403(a) an unauthorized signature is ineffective except as the signature of the unauthorized signer in favor of a person who in good faith pays the instrument or takes it for value. An unauthorized signature may be ratified for all purposes of UCC art. 3.

Nickles explains how in two situations exceptional rules apply to bind the person whose name is signed even though the signature was not authorized. Firstly, when signing "in favor of a person who in good faith pays the instrument or takes it for the value".[12] This is true even if the unauthorized signer uses someone else's name, such as the name of the person who purports to represent. It makes no difference whether or not the signer believes, when he signs, that he is acting for and with the authority of someone else. Secondly, because of extraordinary rules that extend even to cases of outright forgery, a person's unauthorized signature can sometimes bind him for reasons of ratification and culpability of fault.[13]

Another issue to consider is the authority to draw cheques. As a payment system, cheques allow to discharge monetary obligations. Because of this possibility, there is a consensus upon this power for directors. However, such power may be restricted as to a maximum amount of money. Under this latter scenario, it is possible to hold that when a cheque is drawn up to a higher sum of money, the ultra vires doctrine applies. Conversely, a corporation cannot avoid liability on a negotiable bill, note, or bond in the hands of a *bona fide* purchaser by setting up the defense that it is ultra vires because it was issued in violation of a provision limiting the amount of indebtedness which the corporation might incur, or because it was issued for a purpose for which

---

[10] *Moss vs. Averell*, 10 N.Y. 457; *Mechreeseanics Bank vs. White Lead Co.* 35 N.Y. 505. Cit, Brice (1893), p. 251, footnote 2.

[11] Reese (1897) §100. Where a corporation has general authority to issue negotiable notes, a note issued by it for ultra vires purposes, e.g., for purchase of stock in another corporation, is not enforceable by the payee but is good in the hands of a holder in due course. In re Jefferson Bank v. Chapman–White–Lyons Co. 122 Tenn. 415, 123 S.W. 64, Brannan (1926), p. 456. Spanish Negotiable Instruments Law 19/1985, art. 9, presumes that corporate directors are authorized to issue drafts due to their appointment. The same principle applies in Colombia with any kind of negotiable instrument, according to the C.Co. art. 641.

[12] Nickles (1994), 85–86.

[13] See footnote 12.

the corporation was not authorized by its charter to issue it.[14] In the same ratio, if a director is powered to draw a negotiable instrument it is also powered to indorse it under the ancient roman aphorism: "*qui potest plus, potest minus*".[15]

Where a company or its directors have the authority to issue negotiable instruments, this is an absolute and general authority, and it cannot be restricted in degree or amount, subsequent clauses confining the liability of the company or its members to certain sums being repugnant and void. Consequently, bills that have been drawn or notes made under such authority, even in the hands of a holder with notice of the limitation, bind the company both at Law and in Equity. Such a restriction differs *in toto* from the imposition of a formality. A company may well require for its protection that the powers which it confers upon its agents shall be exercisable in certain ways only, and parties dealing with the company will frequently have to see that such formalities are duly observed, but to say that its agents may engage in transactions up to a certain amount only, would be to stipulate that every person entering into any contract with the company shall investigate the state of the company's business.[16]

Another relevant issue concerning to the ultra vires doctrine it was related to corporate power to acquire and hold stock of another corporation. Indeed, in the nineteenth century, American law was settled that in the absence of an express grant in the statute or its charter a corporation had no power to purchase the stock of another corporation.[17] As explained by Blumberg, such acquisition of stock of another corporation was prohibited without regard to whether the other company was conducting a similar business or was in an entirely different one.[18]

The charter of a corporation is the measure of its powers. It can exercise only such powers as are conferred upon it, either in express terms or by necessary implication, in the law of its creation. The purchase of stock in another corporation involves

---

[14] 94 Wood v. Corry Water-Works Co., 44 Fed. 146, 12 L. R. A. 168; Auerbach v. Le Sueur Mill Co., 28 Minn. 291, 9 N. W. 799, 41 Am. Rep. 285. 95 Monument Nat. Bank v. Globe Works, 101 Mass. 57, 3 Am. Rep. 322; Wright v. Pipe Line Co., 101 Pa. St. 204, 4 Ky. L. Rep. 738, 4 Am. Rep. 701; National Bank of Republic v. Young, 41 N. J. Eq. 531, 7 Atl. 488; Credit Co. v. Howe Machine Co., 54 Conn. 357, 8 At. 472, 1 Am. St. Rep. 128. Cf. Ballantine (1930), p. 273.

[15] Whenever a corporation exceeds its powers in taking commercial paper as payee or indorsee, the parties liable on the paper cannot take advantage of that fact as a defense to the action on the paper by the corporation; for, having made the paper payable to the corporation, and received its funds as consideration therefor, the maker, drawer, acceptor or indorser, as the case might be, is estopped from denying the capacity of the corporation to take the paper. See, Reese (1897) §101.

[16] Brice (1893), p. 268. The maker of a note cannot object that a corporate holder purchased the note ultra vires. Prescott Nat'l Bank v. Butler, 157 Mass. 548, 32 N. E. 909 (1893). Neither can the obligor of a non-negotiable choice in action defend on the ground that the plaintiff corporation's purchase was ultra vires. In re John Farwell Co. v. Wolf, 96 Wis. 10, 70 N. W. 289 (1897). *Contra*: Pueblo v. Shutt Co., 28 Colo. 524, 67 Pac. 162 (1901). Cf. Stevens (1927), p. 306, footnote 37. Where an agent has the authority to issue negotiable paper for any purpose, a person receiving it in the ordinary course of business is justified in assuming that it was properly issued. Thus a holder of negotiable paper issued by a corporation that has the power to issue negotiable paper is not affected by the fact that it was issued at a place and for a purpose not authorized by the charter. Vid. Elliott (1911) §215.

[17] Louis Liggett Co. v. Lee, 288 U.S. 517, 556, 589 (1933).

[18] Blumberg (1993), p. 52.

participation in a new and distinct enterprise. A corporation can make such a purchase only when expressly authorized to do so by statute, or when the power can be implied as incidental to the powers specifically granted. That which is beyond the power of a corporation to do in the first instance cannot be made effective by any subsequent act or omission. An ultra vires contract for the purchase of stock by a corporation is void and cannot be validated by estoppel. Corporate purchases of stock have been declared contrary to public policy as well as ultra vires. But where the corporation laws of a State at no time prohibited such purchases by corporations organized thereunder, it was held by a federal court that the enactment, under a new constitution, of laws authorizing such purchases showed that prior acquisitions of stocks by corporations were not against the public policy of the State, even if it did not expressly legalize the particular transactions.[19]

In fact, the operation of the rule that a corporation, without statutory authority, cannot subscribe for or purchase stock in another corporation is in no way affected by the fact that such purchase or subscription may be of benefit to it. An ultra vires agreement is not made intra vires by being profitable. The contract of association cannot be enlarged to take in a new adventure because the transaction seems expedient.[20]

This doctrine was also seen as a necessary barrier to the ready evasion of the restricted business purposes specified in a corporation's charter. Such an action as purchasing stock of another corporation was seen as an improper expansion of the restricted corporate purpose. The courts reasoned that a failure to include the power to purchase shares in the enumeration of corporate powers indicated an intention to exclude it and that such an acquisition was therefore ultra vires. Although the doctrine of ultra vires was frequently advanced as the rationale for the result, the lack of authority rested on a more formidable basis. Thus, in several cases, the corporate charter did expressly include the power, making it impossible to contend that exercise of the power was ultra vires. Nevertheless, courts invalidated stock purchases, reasoning that the inclusion of the power in the charter was unlawful where the corporation statute did not contain such an authorization.[21]

---

[19] Noyes (1909), pp. 473–474. This author notices that in the case of Schofield v. Goodrich Bros. Banking Co., 98 Fed. 273 (1899) the Circuit Court of Appeals for the Eighth Circuit said: "The purchase of the stock of another corporation as an investment and not as security or in payment of a debt, by a corporation simply empowered to do a banking business, is beyond its power and void and since such a purchase is ultra vires and void, it cannot be made good or validated by estoppel".

[20] Noyes (1909), p. 481. In re, Valley R. Co. v. Lake Erie Iron Co., 46 Ohio St. 44 (1888), (18 N. E. Rep. 486, 1 L. R. A. 412, 26 Am. & Eng. Corp. Cas. 56). In re Central R. Co. v. Collins, 40 Ga. 582 (1869) the Supreme Court of Georgia ruled: "We do not think the profitableness of this contract, to the stockholders of the Central and Southwestern Railroad has anything to do with the matter. These stockholders have a rigid, at their pleasure, to stand on their contract. If the charters do not give these companies the right to go into this new enterprise anyone stockholder has a right to object. He is not to be forced into an enterprise not included in the charter. That it will be to his interest is no excuse; that is for him to judge".

[21] Blumberg (1993), p. 53. The Supreme Court has ruled: "But as the powers of corporations, created by legislative act, are limited to such as the act expressly confers, and the enumeration of these implies the exclusion of all others, it follows that, unless express permission is given to do so, it is not within the general powers of a corporation to purchase the stock of other corporations for

Classical corporate theory both narrowed and privatized ultra vires. The corporation has been understood as an entity composed of private persons but created by the state for a public purpose, strict scrutiny of corporate powers and activities seems appropriate. On the other hand, when the corporation is simply an alternative form of business organization, it should be able to do the same things as any other business firm. By the 1880s and 1890s, courts had retreated from the view that a corporation's powers were defined by a strict construction of its charter. They became much more willing to imply authority from other explicit powers. Even the Supreme Court, which usually construed corporate powers narrowly, held in 1896 that the express power granted to a corporation to run a railroad implied the power to operate a hotel, at least if the hotel was for the convenience of railroad passengers and employees.[22]

Reese submits that for a time there was an element of uncertainty appearing in the views expressed by the courts, as to whether or not the doctrine should be applied only to the acts of a corporation, as such, or whether it should not also be applied to acts of the directors or officers which were beyond the authority given them in the management of corporate internal affairs.[23] Only in the former sense is the doctrine legitimately applicable. This rather ambiguous conception of the doctrine led the courts down many avenues of technical reasoning and precipitated discussions of the principles of the law governing the relations of principal and agent, trustee and *cestui que trust*, and principles governing other questions of like nature, which do not properly belong to the doctrine in its application to chartered corporations.[24]

Reviewing all those case law scenarios, scholars made a remembrance about a legislative attempt at codification and restatement of the ultra vires doctrine.[25] Indeed, the Committee on a Uniform Incorporation Act in its report to the Commissioners on Uniform State Laws in 1924 included a provision, as to the effect of ultra vires acts. This ninth tentative draft of a uniform incorporation act was the first to contain any provision concerning the subject of ultra vires. Since there is no other topic where the law is in a more unsatisfactory or confused condition, it seemed that the opportunity for establishing uniformity in this field ought not to be lost. Thus, the s. 7 of the ninth tentative draft reads:

> Section 7. *Corporate Capacity and* Authority.-Sub-division I. Every corporation formed under this Act shall be a body politic and shall be deemed to have the general capacities of a natural person, provided, however, the limits of permissible corporate action shall be those defined and restricted by the articles of incorporation and amendments thereof, and by the provisions of this Act and of the other laws and the Constitution of this State.
>
> *******

---

the purpose of controlling their management". In Re. De La Vergne Refrigerating Machine Co. v. German Savings Ins. 175 U.S. 40, 54–55 (1899).

[22] Hovenkamp (1988), p. 1663.

[23] Reese (1897) §17.

[24] Reese (1897) §17.

[25] Ballantine (1927), pp. 453–454. According to this author, the effort to restore the law to realism on this subject was certainly a timely and courageous one and deserved vigorous support. The main criticism is that it fails to go far enough in indicating what practical legal consequences and changes are intended to be produced. It attempts to repeal an artificial theory or premise, that of limited capacity or powers, and to establish a theory of general capacity or powers.

> Sub-division III. If any acts shall have been done by a corporation in excess of its powers, the corporation's lack of power to do such act shall not be inquired into collaterally, provided that the act is one that the corporation might, at the time the act was committed, have been formed under this Act with power to do. Any action by a corporation in excess of its powers may be enjoined at the suit of any shareholder. The commission by a corporation of any act in excess of its corporate powers shall be a ground for the forfeiture of the corporate existence at the suit of the State, and the directors engaging in such unauthorized corporate action shall be liable to the corporation for any damage suffered thereby in a suit by it, or by a shareholder in case it will not or cannot sue therefor.

Its draftsman, Professor Stevens, authored an Article[26] proclaiming that it seems obvious that given that the ultra vires dilemma is of legislative creation, the key to its solution is in the hands of the legislature. A restatement may influence the courts in shaping case law but cannot do more. The courts cannot effect a complete cure without usurping the function of the legislature. The cure for the ultra vires ailment calls for some legislation and much restatement by the courts. According to this author, despite apparent confusion reigning in the ultra vires doctrine, there are certain propositions as to which there is substantial unanimity among courts and certain propositions which have the support of a majority of the American jurisdictions:

(1) Even when a corporation assumes to engage in an ultra vires business, responsibility will be attached to the corporation for torts committed by its agents, acting within their authority, in the course of doing business.
(2) Even though a corporation has acted outside the scope of its authority in taking or holding title to property, the validity of its title cannot be questioned on the grounds that the corporation was without authority, or exceeded its authority, in taking or holding the property.
(3) Even though a corporation has acted outside the scope of its authority in making a contract, if it has been fully performed on both sides, it will stand as a foundation of rights acquired under it.
(4) When a corporation has acted outside the scope of its authority in making a contract, either the corporation or the other party thereto may set that fact up as a complete defense to any action brought either at law or in equity upon the contract, provided the contract is wholly executory on both sides.
(5) A non-assenting shareholder, unless estopped or barred by his laches, may be granted an injunction to restrain an act threatened to be done on behalf of a corporation when such act would be beyond the scope of corporate authority.
(6) The commission by a corporation of an act outside the scope of the authority conferred upon it does not, of itself, put an end to corporate existence, but

[26] Stevens (1927), p. 289. Such author subsequently wrote a *note* entitled "Statutory Modification of the Doctrine of Ultra Vires" (1930), p. 285, where he concluded that any attempt to reform the ultra vires doctrine a legislature is faced with the necessity of compromising between a statute which changes the law and one which retains the desirable flexibility of the corpus of judicial precedents. Statutes like the Uniform Act, which retain flexibility by the novel device of changing only the theories on which decisions are based, may not cure the defects in the existing law; while the California and Ohio act, although changing the law, may be too rigid.

> furnishes grounds for the forfeiture of the charter of the corporation, or for ousting it from the exercise of the unauthorized powers, upon the state's application in a quo warranto proceeding.

Some courts avoided the ultra vires doctrine by constructing purpose clauses broadly and finding implied purposes from the language used. A famous example is a conclusion by the United States Supreme Court that a railway company might engage in the business of leasing and running a seaside resort hotel.[27] Other adjudications have found acceptance include estoppel, unjust enrichment, quasi-contract, and waiver. In particular, these doctrines were applied to ensure that completed transactions would not be disturbed and to permit tort claimants to recover from injuries suffered as a consequence of the corporation's conduct of an ultra vires business. Such doctrine continued to be applied in connection with executory agreements and when all is said and done, the doctrine was an undesirable one, involving harsh and erratic consequences.[28]

Subsequent reforms were introduced to the Uniform Business Corporation Act (UBCA). In its final form—prior to the 2016 revision—such act distinguished between corporate *capacity* and corporate *authority*. Therefore, a corporation had the capacity or power to act possessed by a natural person. However, it has authority to act only in furtherance of its charter and in accordance with corporate law rules. In more recent years the UBCA and the statutes of many states have gone a step further and specifically provided that the validity of a corporation action may not be challenged on the grounds that it exceeds the corporations' power except in two principal circumstances: (1) a suit by the shareholders to enjoin the corporation from performing the ultra vires act, and (2) a derivative or direct suit against the persons who took the ultra vires action on behalf of the corporation. These changes lessened but not eliminated the importance of the ultra vires concept. Litigants often "throw in" an ultra vires claim in order not to overlook any possible avenue for convincing a court of their position. Occasionally, however, the allocation of loss between insiders and outsiders will turn on the court's understanding and application of the ultra vires doctrine.[29]

As time goes by and bearing in mind massive criticisms arose from academia and businessmen, the ultra vires doctrine was falling into moving sands, and despite trying to refloat, it was continuing to sink. Beyond the interest of the state in the decline of the doctrine, or the shareholders' profit maximization concerns about expanding directors' powers to engage in any lawful—and profitable—activity, the main reason for the doctrine's downfall was based on unscrupulous people using it to elude their obligations and cheat creditors' rights. Indeed, the ultra vires doctrine eroded as the rationales for its existence became less important and the costs of enforcing the doctrine grew. Initially, the firmest pressure to eliminate the doctrine came from suppliers and other creditors of the corporation, as they began to be the doctrine's victims rather than its beneficiaries. In some jurisdictions, corporations

---

[27] Jacksonville M. P. Ry. & Nav. Co. v. Hooper, 160 U.S. 514, 16 S.Ct. 379, 40 L.Ed. 515 (1896).

[28] Hamilton (2005), p. 224.

[29] O'Kelley (2010), pp. 687–688.

themselves began to use the doctrine as a defense to contract actions against them, thereby avoiding obligations into which they had freely entered.[30]

Nowadays the MBCA and their latest version, the Revised Model Business Corporation Act 2016 (MBCA–2016) provides in §3.01:

(a) Every corporation incorporated under this act has the purpose of engaging in any lawful business unless a more limited purpose is set forth in the articles of incorporation.
(b) A corporation engaging in a business that is subject to regulation under another statute of this state may incorporate under this act only if permitted by, and subject to all limitations of, the other statute.

This is the official comment of such a provision:

> The choice of an 'any lawful business' clause has become nearly universal in states that permit the clause. Even if the articles of incorporation limit lines of business in which the corporation may engage, the limited scope of the ultra vires concept in litigation between the corporation and outsiders means that a third person entering into a transaction that violates the restrictions in the purpose clause may be able to enforce the transaction in accordance with its terms if the third person was unaware of the narrow purpose clause when entering into the transaction.
>
> Many corporations may also find it desirable to supplement a general purpose clause with an additional statement of business purposes. This may be necessary for licensing or for qualification or registration purposes in some states.
>
> Section 3.01(b) recognizes that certain state statutes may preclude incorporation under the Act or limit the purpose of or otherwise regulate the business or affairs of corporations formed to, or actually engaging in, certain lines of business.
>
> - Some of these statutes, particularly those relating to banking and insurance, establish a separate incorporation process and incorporating agency. These special incorporating statutes may refer to or incorporate by reference portions of the Act. Other statutes provide for incorporation for the purpose of practicing a profession.
> - Other statutes may permit incorporation under the Act if the corporation imposes restrictions or limitations in its articles of incorporation; these restrictions may relate to the business in which the corporation may engage, its manner of internal governance, or the persons who may or may not be shareholders and participate in the venture. The language of Section 3.01(b) is designed to cover all these multiple variations.
> - Other types of entities, such as nonprofit corporations, cooperatives, and unions, usually may not incorporate under the Act. Special statutes may apply to these entities, such as the Model Nonprofit Corporation Act.[31]

[30] Greenfield (2001), p. 1310. A long time ago, civil law jurisdictions adopted as a principle the roman aphorism: *nemo auditor propriam turpitudinem allegans*, this means that nobody can invoke his fault or negligence to get a personal benefit. This rule avoids a person obtaining a favorable result for himself or a third party, based on an anomalous act such as contract transaction or tortious conduct when the irregularity arises from his negligence or intentional wrong behavior. See, Díez-Picazo (1963), pp. 39–40.

[31] www.americanbar.org/content/dam/aba/administrative/business_law/corplaws/2016_mbca.authcheckdam.pdf [last accessed: 12/Sep/2021].

Taking into account such a norm, why would articles of incorporation today ever include a narrow purposes clause? There are some explanations: (i) some types of corporations may be engaged in business subject to state regulation that permits incorporation under general business statutes, but requires limitations on certain types of corporate activities; (ii) some persons may be uncomfortable with the complete lack of useful information about the purpose of the corporation, preferring that some description of the principal business appear in the articles of association; (iii) in closely-held corporations, a limited purposes clause may be used where one or more persons interested in the corporation wish to restrict the line of business the corporation may enter into.[32]

Because of the Covid-19 pandemic, in March 2020, the President of the United States invoked the Defense Production Act of 1950 and ordered General Motors Co. (GM) to manufacture ventilators for the treatment of critical patients. GM is an automaker known worldwide and jointly with its partner, Ventec Life Systems, produced these medical devices (ventilators) as of April 2020. GM would operate as a contract manufacturer for Ventec, which would sell and distribute the machines. Beyond the health contingency or the presidential order, GM could manufacture ventilators and automobiles simultaneously without falling into an ultra vires act, because as it reads in its certificate of incorporation:

> The purpose of the Corporation is to engage in *any lawful act or activity* for which corporations may be organized under the General Corporation Law of the State of Delaware[33] (italics added).

As we can notice this clause is a practical application of literal (a) §3.01 MBCA–2016, that allows corporations to engage in any lawful business unless a more limited purpose is outlined in the articles of incorporation.

A provocative theory about the survival of the ultra vires doctrine has been recently exposed by Greenfield, who advocates for the doctrine's living conditions.[34] According to this author, notwithstanding the many strong reasons for the downfall of the doctrine, it did not erode to nothingness. Rather, an important part was retained and survives today. This vestige of the doctrine sets off illegal activities as ultra vires for corporations. In the opinion of Greenfield, the fact that almost any state in the USA and the MBCA contains a provision pointing out that every corporation incorporated under such Act has the purpose of engaging in any lawful business, this, therefore, allows him to conclude that when the act or transaction is not lawful, it consequently becomes ultra vires.

In addition, Greenfield holds to his theory arguing that another piece of evidence demonstrating that some vestige of the ultra vires doctrine survives, is that 49 states still have a provision in their state incorporation statutes that allows the state to dissolve a corporation or enjoin it from engaging in ultra vires activities.[35] These

---

[32] Hamilton (2005), p. 213.

[33] https://www.sec.gov/Archives/edgar/data/1467858/000119312510279214/dex32.htm [last accessed: 12/Sep/2021].

[34] Greenfield (2001), p. 1314.

[35] Greenfield (2001), p. 1319.

provisions are premised, according to Schaeftler, "on the notion that the state had an interest in deterring [ultra vires] activity by virtue of its responsibility to protect the public welfare".[36] One critic has called these provisions statutory 'dead wood', and, indeed, if corporations could genuinely be chartered for any purpose whatsoever these provisions would be meaningless. On the other hand, if a limitation on illegal acts is considered a real constraint, then these provisions are anything but refusals. They recognize that the state continues to have a real interest in ensuring that corporations stay within their stated power and authority, that is, conducting their business lawfully.[37]

Under the same analytic sequence, Greenfield argues that any firm that did not have a term in their corporate contract making illegal acts ultra vires, it would then be expected to have to pay creditors and suppliers more for their inputs to compensate them for the increase in risk arising from the absence of such an ultra vires term.[38] In the alternative, firms without such terms would have to do something to bond their honesty and lawful performance. In this way, a corporation that included in its charter an ultra vires term for illegal activities would likely find that transactions with creditors and suppliers would be less costly than for a corporation that did not have such a term in its charter.[39]

3.2 United Kingdom

As in the USA, in the UK the ultra vires doctrine has been repelled in a major way. It is so that a certain author claims that it "... has bedeviled company law for over a century and in a ghastly way continues to do so despite various efforts of the legislature to ameliorate it...".[40] The same aversion has been shown by the judges; nevertheless, "the judges saw it as their role to fight a rearguard action against these attempts to undermine the ultra vires doctrine, perhaps seeing it as the strongest weapon they had to cope with cases of blatant corporate wrongdoing. They protested frequently at the length and prolixity of the drafting ... and a rather unbecoming attitude for them to take, since most of them must, as counsel, have spent much professional time earlier on in their careers in drafting and settling the very terms which they now sought to condemn!".[41]

The insiders consistently aimed to ensure that the capacity of their companies should be as nearly unfettered as possible. Besides enumerating objects at great length, draftsmen adopted other devices, such as: (i) specifying what are essentially

[36] Schaeftler (1983), p. 85.

[37] Greenfield (2001) p. 1319.

[38] Greenfield (2001), p. 1345.

[39] See footnote 38.

[40] Pettet (2012), p. 144.

[41] Sealy (2013), p. 88.

powers as objects of the company (*Re Introductions Ltd.* [1970] Ch 199, CA (indicating that the courts might not always be persuaded and might, despite the express words, construe the powers as merely incidental) and *Rolled Steel Products (Holdings) Ltd. v British Steel Corpn* [1986] Ch 246, CA); (ii) including clauses designed to ensure that no listed object should be construed restrictively by being read as merely ancillary to some other object (an all objects are 'main objects' clause: see *Cotman v. Brougham* [1918] AC 514, HL); and (iii) authorizing the company, or its directors, to determine any extensions to the company's objects as may seem warranted (a 'subjective objects' clause: see *Bell Houses Ltd. v. City Wall Properties Ltd.* [1966] 2 QB 656, CA): that is, "To carry on any other trade or business whatsoever which can, in the opinion of the board of directors, be advantageously carried out by the company in connection with or as ancillary to ... the general business of the company". Despite attracting judicial complaints, these drafting devices went a considerable way to mitigate the harshness of the ultra vires rule by minimizing the occasions when it could be invoked.[42]

Dignam explains that historically three issues combined to make the ultra vires doctrine a tricky problem for English courts: (i) initially the objects clause was unalterable and then only alterable in limited circumstances until 1989; (ii) unlike public bodies whose functions are relatively fixed, registered companies often did change the central nature of their business; (iii) the doctrine of constructive notice could combine with the ultra vires doctrine to leave unwary third parties with unenforceable contracts.[43]

Investors create corporations to pursue a specific range of activities, and thus one logical way to ensure that a company does not engage in activities other than those intended is to specify a "corporate purpose" or a "corporate object" in the constitutional documents and hold the company to such purpose or object. In this way, the company has a restriction on its *capacity*. In consequence, actions beyond the delegated powers (ultra vires) would be without capacity and therefore void. In the 19th century, this was a common way for investors to put a leash on company management. As Ferran has observed,[44] accounting rules and stock exchange disclosure requirements came to provide investors with more information about company operations, and, with "the investor demand for information met in other ways, the objects clause became, at least potentially, more of a hindrance than a help to investors because it could prevent companies from diversifying their business into more profitable lines

---

[42] Sealy (2013), p. 88. It must be noted, in addition, that draftsmen sometimes preceded the leading objects with the words 'as an independent object' or drafted the leading objects very widely. A further development which has taken place is the appearance of so-called subjective objects clauses. These provide for the carrying on of any business which the company or the directors think fit. The clause in the *Stephenson* case was an example. A common clause is 'To do all such other things as the company may think conducive to the attainment of the above objects or any of them'. Such a clause was accepted in *Peruvian Rlys Co.* (1867) 2 Ch App 617 at 624. Cf. Farrar (1998), p. 102.

[43] Dignam (2012), p. 245.

[44] Ferran (1999), pp. 85–86.

of activity".[45] Investor monitoring and ex post action came to replace an ex ante contractual limitation as to the most effective source of controlling management. Moreover, limiting the activities of a company through its objects can have an unfair impact on third parties. This could, for example, allow a company to enter into a risky agreement in an area beyond its power, and, if the deal turned out to be unprofitable, any shareholder could then sue to have the contract declared void as ultra vires.[46]

In an attempt to further simplify this area, the Company Law Review Steering Group proposed the repeal of the CA 1985 s. 3A, together with the removal of the objects clause from a company's memorandum and insertion into the articles of association.[47] However, CA 2006 went further affording that unless a company's articles specifically restrict its objects, then according to s. 31(1) its objects are unrestricted. Consequently, for companies formed under the new Act, they are not required to have an objects clause and the ultra vires doctrine (as outlined below) should be irrelevant to their operation. Nevertheless, for a company that adopts an objects clause to limit the company's capacity, then the ultra vires doctrine will remain relevant internally, i.e., to deciding whether its directors have exceeded their powers and entered into a transaction that is ultra vires to the company's objects clause.

It is also worth noting at this point that CA 2006 s. 28(1) lays out that provisions within the memorandum of existing companies, i.e., formed before the new Act came into force, which falls outside those envisaged by the new Act, will be treated as provisions of the articles. In other words, provisions such as their objects clause will still form part of the company's constitution as defined by s. 17, and, as such, will be subject to the limitations outlined in the preceding paragraph.

---

[45] Professor Ferran (2014), p. 305, points out that: "an unlawful return of capital is ultra vires. In the quotation from the *Ridge Securities* case, Pennycuick describes the disposition as being ultra vires the company. Ultra vires is an appropriate term in this context because the disposition is contrary to what companies are permitted to do under the general law. Thus in *MacPherson v European Strategic Bureau Ltd 34* an arrangement involving payments to shareholders that were described as payments for consultancy services, which was entered into at a time when the company was insolvent, was held to be ultra vires (…)". However, Ferran notices that: "Ultra vires, in this wide sense, is to be distinguished from ultra vires in the sense of actions falling outside the scope of a company's stated objects. Historically, the ultra vires rule in the latter sense was used by the courts as a creditor protection device, in addition to the rule prohibiting the return of capital to shareholders" Ibid.

[46] Cahn (2010), pp. 313–314.

[47] However, CA 1985, s. 35 did not abolish the ultra vires doctrine at all but simply protected a limited class of person dealing with the company. The company itself could not rely on it. In order to be protected the person had to (1) be dealing with the company, (2) be in good faith, and (3) the transaction had to be decided on by the directors. These three requirements gave rise to a number of problems of interpretation. It was not clear whether a broad or a narrow meaning was to be given to the word 'dealing'. Dealing normally predicates reciprocity and is capable of limitation to commercial transactions. It can also be used in an extended sense. *The Jenkins Report* limited the protection to persons contracting with the company but art. 9 simply talks about third parties in general. There is no reference to dealing. Probably the better view is that 'dealing' was used in an extended sense. See, Farrar (1998), p. 109.

In turn, the subject matter related to the company's capacity is ruled in the CA 2006 s. 39. This provision intended to eliminate the effect of the ultra vires doctrine on the claims of creditors, though it has less of an impact today than it would have had in the past since, fewer transactions are likely to be ultra vires at common law. However, on the assumption that the narrow scope of a particular company's objects clause may still allow for this, a review of certain statutory provisions appears below. It is submitted that the reforms made over the past 30 years (CA 1985 and CA 2006) have deprived the ultra vires doctrine of its central role, but it has not disappeared altogether.[48]

We shall deal at this stage only with the effect of legislation upon the rules relating to the company's capacity because as Smith notices, it should also be borne in mind that legislation only reforms the ultra vires rule and it has not been abolished, though so far as trade creditors of a company are concerned little should now be heard of it. There is a continuing relevance of the rule in other areas.[49]

For reasons of both equity and commercial reality, in the early 20th century, courts began reading object clauses broadly and implying additional powers as necessary. Later, legislatures eliminated the use of ultra vires to void transactions with third parties, while retaining the ability of shareholders to hold management to such restrictions as a matter of internal governance. As a result, even if a company acts beyond its capacity as provided for in the constitutional documents, the laws will uphold the rights of the third party against the corporation arising out of the transaction. Complaints based on ultra vires remain available only for internal actions against directors that act beyond the powers granted to them.[50]

3.3 Australia

Modern Australian company law is grounded in English company law. When companies legislation, along with the English model, were passed in several of the Australian colonies, this was largely done to accommodate the needs of English businesses who wished to set up subsidiaries in Australia or alternatively to register as 'foreign' corporations. There was virtually no demand for company legislation from the domestic industry, which was almost universally small scale. There was, however, one exception to this. The one form of domestic business which required corporate identity and the capacity this gave it to raise funds from the public was the mining industry.

[48] Sealy (2013), p. 87.

[49] Smith (2016), p. 95.

[50] Cahn (2010), pp. 314–315. On the 'internal purposes', the abolition of the traditional connection between a company's objects clause and its capacity does not mean that those acting on behalf of the company now have *carte blanche* to do whatever they wish in the company's name. A member has always had a right to seek an injunction to prevent the company from entering into what would have been an ultra vires transaction. And directors must observe any limitations on their powers flowing from the company's constitution (CA 2006 s. 171) and will be liable to the company for any breaches. Cf. Sealy (2013), p. 90.

The colonial legislation introduced in 1860 following the English model almost word for word. It is not surprising that this was the case, given the integration of Australian and English business interests at the time. Even in respect to the needs of the mining industry, it was not surprising that this was the case, given that many of the investors in the larger mining undertakings would be English and thus would want their investments in entities that were formed on the English model (i.e., limited liability incorporation).[51]

In the eighties, Australian company law literature showed a special interest in the ultra vires doctrine because of the promulgation of two key laws concerning this subject matter: the Companies Code 1981, and subsequently, the Companies and Securities Legislation Act 1983.[52] Under the 1983 legislation, there were substantial amendments to s. 37, 67, and 68 of the Companies Code 1981, which were to operate on and from 1 January 1984. The provision in s. 37 which required a company to state its objects in its memorandum of association, was repealed and replaced by s. 37(1A) which provides that it is now optional for companies to state objects. Section 67 (powers) and s. 68 (ultra vires transactions) were replaced by new provisions.

Despite the manifested purpose to abolish the ultra vires doctrine, the 1983 amendments would result in a wider application of it than the previous legislation. Conversely, other legal writers pointed out that the doctrine was abolished where the memorandum of a company does not state the company's objects and neither the memorandum nor the articles restrict nor prohibit the exercise by the company of any of the powers referred to by law. Thus, if there is either or both a statement of objects in the memorandum or a restriction on or a prohibition of the exercise of the powers in the memorandum or the articles, the doctrine survives to some extent.

Upon this ground, the 1985 legislature finally proposed abolishing the ultra vires doctrine, and without affecting the validity of the company's dealings with outsiders, ensuring that provisions of the rules of a company relating to objects of powers are adhered to by the company's officers and members.[53]

In 1998 the Company Law Review Act was enacted, which inserted the new Part 2B.1—Company powers and how they are exercised. Afterward some criticisms,[54] continuous legislation enacted back in the 20th century, alongside turbulent constitutional adjudications,[55] Australian company law suffered radical changes introduced by the Corporations Act 2001, that led to think that the ultra vires doctrine was abolished by the combined effect of s. 124 and s. 125. According to this interpretation, the doctrine could only have an application to a company whose constitution contained an objects clause or other self-imposed restriction or prohibition on the exercise of its powers. Thus, the Corporations Act 2001 now does not require a company to have an

---

[51] McQueen (1992), pp. 6–7. Also see, Leigh (1970). A comprehensive research about the influence of Great Britain in Australian's company law in McQueen (2009).

[52] See generally: Wilkin (1984), Cain (1985), Sikkema (1985), Pennington (1987), Egert (1991).

[53] Watson (1990), Baxt (1991a), Grantham (1991), Stevenson (1991), Griggs (1993), Woodward (1997).

[54] Baxt (1991b), Dharmananda (1991), Sneddon (1992).

[55] New South Wales v. Commonwealth (1989) 169 CLR 482.

objects clause in its constitution.[56] Indeed, as noted by Lipton as a result of the 1998 amendments, a company does not even need a constitution as the replaceable rules may govern its internal management.[57] To accredit this assertion, it is imperative to study the content and scope of both sections to determine if the ultra vires doctrine was abolished. Firstly, s. 124 provides:

Legal capacity and powers of a company:

(1) A company has the legal capacity and powers of an individual both in and outside this jurisdiction. A company also has all the powers of a body corporate, including the power to:

(…)

(h) do anything that it is authorized to do by any other law (including a law of a foreign country).

(…)

(2) A company's legal capacity to do something is not affected by the fact that the company's interests are not, or would not be, served by doing it.

(3) For the avoidance of doubt, this section does not:

(a) authorize a company to do an act that is prohibited by a law of a State or Territory; or

(b) give a company a right that a law of a State or Territory denies the company.

The approach took in s. 124 confers broad powers on a company; however, not all corporations have such broad powers. In the case of many statutory corporations, their powers will be confined to doing acts in connection with the purpose for which they were chartered. For example, the Australian Securities and Investment Commission (ASIC) is a body corporate, and its powers are limited to "whatever is necessary for or in connection with, or reasonably incidental to, the performance of its functions". Therefore, if ASIC attempted to do something that was not necessary for the performance of its functions, that act would be of no legal effect by operation of the ultra vires doctrine.[58]

A first criticism about the redaction of this section has to deal with the fact that, ab initio, wrongly proclaims that companies have the legal capacity and powers of an *individual*. From an ontological, philosophic, and legal view, it is not correct to

---

[56] The current legal term "constitution" has to deal with the company's constituent documents (memorandum of association and articles of association) which are no longer required since in effect the Company Law Review Act 1998. Some reasons to adopt a constitution in Hanrahan (2008), 4–520.

[57] Lipton (2008), p. 89.

[58] Hanrahan (2008), p. 456. Before January 1, 1984, the companies did not have the broad-ranging powers now conferred on them by Corporations Act 2001, s. 124. Then, companies only had power to do what was necessary for, connective with, or incidental to the attainment of particular purposes set out in the company's memorandum of association. In order to confer upon companies the widest possible capacity, it became the practice of lawyers to draft long objects clauses, dealing with every possible activity they could imagine, for inclusion in the company's memorandum. Op. cit., footnote 8.

claim this asseveration. Corporations only have the legal capacity and powers in accordance with their nature as a 'moral person'.[59] Likewise, it seems tautological to state that the company has the power to "(h) do anything that it is authorized to do by any other law (including a law of a foreign country)". It is so because one law cannot authorize something that had been previously authorized by another law that is still in effect.

On the other hand, according to num. (2) ibid.: "A company's legal capacity to do something is not affected by the fact that the company's interests are not, or would not be, served by doing it". This provision has a historical background. Aforetime, some courts would reason that the contract celebrated or executed by the company beyond its powers (ultra vires) might not be in accordance with its "best" interest, in that respect, the act cannot be enforced. According to Chapple, the use of the expression 'best' interests in the former provision is too restricting because of the strong association between the "best interests" of the company and the directors' fiduciary duties. Thus, the new s. 124(2) makes it clearer that capacity is not affected by any non-corporate purpose, not just the directors' breach of fiduciary duty.[60]

Taking into account the broad wording of s. 124 (1) and (2), the third numeral contemplates that for the sake of clarity, this section does not: (a) authorize a company to do an act that is prohibited by a State or Territorial law; or (b) give a company a right that a law of a State or Territory denies them. In this respect, the ancient hermeneutical principle applies that a previous restrictive law prevails over a later, more general one. Furthermore, Corporations Act 2001 makes clear that it does not grant a right denied by some other jurisdiction. Thus, the firm's rights are exclusively circumscribed to all those contained in the new legislation. In turn, it could be assumed, that from an integrated reading of both s. 124 and s. 125, the ultra vires doctrine was abolished. To verify this assertion, let us examine s. 125:

> Constitution may limit powers and set out objects:
>
> (1) If a company has a constitution, it may contain an express restriction on, or a prohibition of, the company's exercise of any of its powers. The exercise of power by the company is not invalid merely because it is contrary to an express restriction or prohibition in the company's constitution.
>
> (2) If a company has a constitution, it may set out the company's objects. An act of the company is not invalid merely because it is contrary to or beyond any objects in the company's constitution.

While not compulsory, it is important to restrict the exercise of the company's powers as it is pointed out in s. 125(1) ab initio. This kind of restriction may be from

---

[59] It is possible to conceive that s. 124(1) is differently worded from the former s. 161 in two respects. First, the granting of power to the company is "the legal capacity and powers of an individual" whereas previously it was "legal capacity of a natural person". No significance is attributed to this change. However, former s. 161(2) made the granting of power "subject to the Law". This qualification was deleted, with the result that the breach of any provision of the Corporations Act 2001 cannot affect the company's legal capacity. This effect is important and overrules any past arguments as to the effect of illegal transactions. Vid. Chapple (2002), p. 68.

[60] Chapple (2002), p. 68.

financial activities such as a maximum amount of money to contract to delegate the engagement of a board of directors to a recruiter. Unfortunately, as stated in the same provision, *in fine*, the exercise of power by the company is not invalid *merely* because it is contrary to an express restriction or prohibition in the company's constitution. In this way, it makes no sense to insert such a provision into the company's constitution, if, at the end of the day, it cannot be asserted to third parties.[61]

In the opinion of Hanrahan, the fact that a company has such broad powers may not suit all of its participants.[62] Therefore, those stakeholders may agree among themselves that the company will limit its activities in certain ways. By including such restrictions in the company's constitution, those restrictions will bind not only those who adhere to them at the time but also the company and any person who becomes a member or officer of the company at a later time because a company's constitution operates as a statutory contract binding on all its participants, under s. 140.[63]

The Corporations Act 2001 also determined that it was non-compulsory to set out the company's objects. Thus, such provision—125(2)—may be the cornerstone to support the opinion of the abolishing of the ultra vires doctrine in Australia. It is rightly so because the doctrine rests upon an act executed beyond the corporate's powers, and if those powers were not set out through the company objects, then it is not possible to exceed it. Moreover, this new legislation also established that an act of the company is not invalid *merely* because it is contrary to or beyond any objects in the company constitution. Similarly, to explain the last commentary about s. 124, it makes no sense to insert this provision in the company constitution because it does not have validity even when the company has enacted it in its constitution.

It is submitted that the intention of both sections—125(1) and 125(2)—is to abolish the ultra vires doctrine as it applies to companies so that third parties that deal with companies can enforce obligations incurred by companies, even where those obligations were incurred in breach of these internal restrictions. However, there can be consequences resulting from acts that are outside restrictions in the company's constitution. Such acts may amount to a breach of the statutory contract represented by the company constitution. Causing the company to do something inconsistent with these restrictions may also amount to a breach of duty or other wrongful conduct on the part of the person (such as a director) who caused the company to do the act, and consequences may result from such a breach.[64]

---

[61] The effect of s. 125 is similar to former s. 162 by expressly providing that the exercise of power is not invalid merely because it contravenes the constitution. However, the streamlined s. 125 may confuse as it no longer makes the indirect or internal effects of a breach of the constitution transparent. Contravention of the constitution may still be raised in related actions such as prosecutions of directors, actions for damages against directors, oppression proceedings, and winding up applications. Section 125 may be misleading as it no longer recognizes these effects, despite still existing. Cf. Chapple (2002), p. 68.

[62] Hanrahan (2008), pp. 22–160.

[63] See footnote 62.

[64] Hanrahan (2008), p. 457. Both sections—125(1) and 125(2)—provide that the exercise of a power or act of a company is not invalid merely because it is outside the restrictions imposed by

Contraventions of a company constitution may have other consequences even though they cannot affect the validity of the company's contracts. Allegations that a company acted contrary to its objects or other restrictions or prohibitions in the company's constitution may be an element in legal actions against the company directors for breach of duty. A failure to comply with the constitution may also be contrary to the interests of members as a whole or oppressive and allow a member to seek a remedy. It may also allow a member to obtain an order for the winding-up of the company on a just and equitable ground.[65]

References

Ballantine H (1927) Proposed revision of the ultra vires doctrine. Cornell L Rev 12(4)
Ballantine H (1930) Manual of Corporations law, Chicago
Baxt (1991a) Ultra vires—has it been revived? Company and Securities L J 1:101
Baxt (1991b) Company law reform—the future and fixing up the past—the doctrine of ultra vires. Australian Bus L Rev 19:147
Blumberg P (1993) The multinational challenge to corporation law: the search for a new corporate personality, New York
Brannan J (1926) Negotiable instruments law, Cincinnati
Brice S (1893) A treatise on the doctrine of ultra vires, London
Cahn A et al (2010) Comparative company law, New York
Cain (1985) Ultra vires in 1984. Qld Inst Tech L J 1:31
Chapple L et al (2002) Corporate authority and dealings with officers and agents, Melbourne
Dharmananda (1991) Ultra vires goes ultra violet. Australian L J 71:622
Díez-Picazo L (1963) Doctrina de los Propios Actos, Barcelona
Dignam A et al (2012) Company law, Oxford
Egert (1991) The doctrine of ultra vires—recent developments. Qld U Tech L J 2:73
Elliott C (1911) Treatise on the law of private corporations, Indianapolis
Farrar J et al (1998) Company law, London
Ferran E (1999) Company law and corporate finance, New York
Ferran E et al (2014) Principles of corporate finance law, Oxford
Grantham (1991) Ultra vires: gone but not forgotten, Australian Bar Rev 10:233
Greenfield K (2001) Ultra vires lives! Virginia L Rev 7:87
Griggs et al (1993) Wider ultra vires—reincarnation of a former ghost. Australian Bar Rev 10:176
Hamilton R et al (2005) Corporations, St. Paul
Hanrahan P (2008) Commercial applications of company law, Sydney
Holdsworth (1922) History of English law, vol 1. Boston
Holmes O (1923) The common law, Boston
Hovenkamp H (1988) The classical corporation in american legal thought. Georgetown L J 76(5)
Leigh (1970) Objects, power and ultra vires. Modern L Rev 33:81
Lipton P et al (2008) Understanding company law, Sydney
McQueen R (1992) Australian corporate law and regulation: 1901–1961. UNSW L J 15
McQueen R (2009) A social history of company law, Farnham

the constitution. This suggests that other conduct of a person dealing with a company may affect the validity of the act. In particular, if a person dealing with a company has been aware that the act was inconsistent with the restriction contained in the constitution, any contract may be voidable as against that person at the option of the company. Op. cit., footnote 10.

[65] Lipton (2008), p. 89.

Nickles S et al (1994) Modern commercial paper, St. Paul

Noyes W (1909) A treatise on the law of intercorporate relations, Boston

O'Kelley C et al (2010) Corporations and other business associations, New York

Pennington (1987) Reform of the ultra vires rule. Company Lawyer 8:103

Pettet B (2012) Company law, Harlow

Plucknett T (1956) History of the common law, London

Pound R (1931) The spirit of common law, Boston

Reese R (1897) the doctrine of ultra vires, Chicago

Sealy L et al (2013) Cases and materials in company law, Oxford

Schaeftler M (1983) Ultra vires—ultra useless. J Corp L 9:81

Sikkema (1985) Ultra vires—like phoenix arisen from its ashes. Company and Securities L J 3:16

Smith et al (2016) Company law, Harlow

Sneddon (1992) Protection of financiers from ultra vires and related defenses. L Inst J 66:70

Stevens R (1927) A proposal as to the codification and restatement of the ultra vires doctrine. Yale L J 36(3)

Stevens R (1930) Statutory modification of the doctrine of ultra vires. Harvard L Rev 44(2)

Stevenson (1991) Ultra vires doctrine: is it dead? Melbourne

Watson (1990) Corporate collapse: time to reintroduce the ultra vires rule? Company and Securities L J 8:240

Wilkin (1984) Ultra vires is alive, well and living in Australia. L Inst J 58:256

Woodward (1997) Ultra vires oversimplified: changes to company powers under the second Corporations law simplification bill. Company and Securities L J 15:162

Chapter 4
The Ultra Vires Doctrine in European Civil Law

Abstract In this chapter and the next one, there is a presentation of the ultra vires doctrine in the main civil law jurisdictions, both Europe (France, Germany, Italy and, Spain) and Latin America (Argentina, Brasil, Colombia, México, and Perú). This is a key research point of this monograph because explores the way that diverse legal systems, have adopted the concept of corporate capacity as an attribute of the moral entities' personality, and the adverse consequences when acting either exceeding it or with the lack of it.

4.1 Introduction

Schlesinger points out that "unlike most other subjects in law school curriculums, comparative law is not a body of rules and principles. It is primarily a *method*, a way of looking at legal problems, legal institutions, and entire legal systems. By the use of comparison as a method, it becomes possible to make observations and gain insights that would be denied to one whose study is limited to the law of a single country. Neither the comparative method, nor the insights gained through its use, can be said to constitute a body of binding norms, or a distinct branch of law, in the sense in which we speak of the law of contracts or torts. In this respect, the term comparative law is a misnomer. It would be more accurate to speak of comparison of laws and legal systems. However, by the force of tradition, the term Comparative Law has become the accepted title of both handbooks and subjects in law schools across diverse legal systems (common law and civil law)".[1] To get involved in academic research on comparative law represents a true challenge, which gets harder when it comes to corporate law. Although the business world tends to unify, the legal environment, to the contrary, seems quite reluctant to follow this track. This is mainly due to both political issues and the reverence given to tradition rather than a practical issue.

---

[1] Schlesinger (1998), p. 2.

M. A. Jiménez Sánchez, *The Ultra Vires Doctrine in Corporate Law*, SpringerBriefs in Law, https://doi.org/10.1007/978-3-030-88838-1_4

The corporation has been a remarkably resilient legal institution for two hundred years of industrialization and modernization, largely because of its capacity to adapt constantly to a changing environment. Legal systems that have facilitated this process of adaptation and were able to respond to new legal lacunae created by the change have proved to be more successful over time. From the perspective of legal innovation, common law countries have been more successful than civil law countries, and origin countries have been more successful than transplant countries.[2] This evolutionary process was experienced intensely in Europe because despite having common roots, each nation developed an autonomous legal framework. However, huge efforts were made to get the unification of the most prominent class of company: the joint-stock company.[3]

Indeed, the EEC Member States share common legal characteristics because Roman Law sources permeated them. However, the harmonization of company law has encountered the hardship that certain legal concepts may be familiar in one member state, but unfamiliar and hard to understand in another. The best example is the theory of the company "organs" which is used in the First Directive in relation to ultra vires transactions. This concept is familiar in Germany and some other Member States but is not in the UK or Ireland.[4] Under this context, it is appropriate to point out that another field in which the communitarian lawmakers have enacted is about the company's power of representation and the objects clause. On one side, the faculty to bind the firm and the enforceability of the director's subjective limitations (delegation, joint representation, board or by-laws limits to directors and officers). On the other hand, the objective scope of those powers concerning the contract and third parties. Thus, according to Directive 68/151/EEC, art. 8:

> Completion of the formalities of disclosure of the particulars concerning the persons who, as an organ of the company, are authorized to represent it shall constitute a bar to any irregularity in their appointment being relied upon as against third parties unless the company proves that such third parties had knowledge thereof.

La Villa explains that whether the national law legislates that the power of representation may be allotted to one individual, or jointly to various persons, the same law

[2] Pistor (2002), pp. 793–794.

[3] See, García (2002). According to art. 1 of the Council Regulation No. 2157/2001 on the Statute for a European Company: (1) A company may be set up within the territory of the community in the form of a European public limited-liability company (*Societas Europaea* or SE) on the conditions and in the manner established in this Regulation; (2) The capital of an SE shall be divided into shares. No shareholder shall be liable for more than the amount he has subscribed; (3) An SE shall have legal personality; (4) Employee involvement in an SE shall be governed by the provisions of Directive 2001/86/EC.

[4] Andenas (2009), p. 39. By comparison, the EU harmonization in company law differs in many aspects. One difference is that the harmonization typically has been mandatory in the form of directives. The mandatory nature of the directives comes in two forms. Either the directive or part of it is based on minimum rules, where the Member States must at least fulfill the minimum requirement and only allow for national solutions above the minimum rule, or it is based on maximum-minimum rules, which leave little room for national solutions or no room at all for national solutions for the Member States. Vid. Andersson (2015), pp. 36–37.

might establish that this clause is enforceable against a third party if the exception relates to "general power" to represent the corporation.[5]

Another chief aspect dealing with the Directive is the objects clause. According to a first tendency, the objects clause confines the firm's capacity, in this way, any act outside the corporate purpose is void because of the want of capacity. This is the motto of Anglo-American ultra vires doctrine followed by some French jurists and judges, who considered that taking into account the government authorization to corporations to operate, all of the acts executed beyond the given powers cannot be considered lawful. In this respect, only the acts performed following charter and by-laws may be cataloged as legitimate.[6] The second is a German tendency. According to this perspective, the directors are not obligated due to the objects clause. Consequently, they have exclusive power to manage the corporation in its best interest, and only exceptionally, the lack of power may be opposable to third party when both the director and such a third party engage in a collusion strategy to harm the corporate interests.

Based on this, an eclectic theory arose. According to it, when an act goes beyond company capacity because it is beyond the objects clause, it must be considered as carried out by an unauthorized representative. Thusly, it would not be considered *invalid* but rather *ineffective* and would need to be expressly ratified by the company. This exception of excess of the objects clause can only be argued for the company and prohibited to the third party since it remains in the ambit of unauthorized representation. It must be kept in mind that the faculty to reject the act is attributed to the represented, i.e., the company, not to third party.[7]

Bearing in mind the discrepancies in ancient and modern common law about the nature, scope, application, and effects derivate from the ultra vires doctrine, The Council of the EC enacted the First Council Directive [68/151/EEC]. As stressed in the preamble, the coordination of national provisions concerning disclosure, the validity of obligations, entered into by, and the nullity of such companies is of special importance, particularly for protecting the interests of third parties. Sánchez contended that because of the existence of one common market, it was necessary to eliminate disturbing legal differences between the Member States to guarantee valid contract relationships.[8] Therefore art. 9(1) provides:

---

[5] La Villa (1996), pp. 44–45.

[6] It is interesting the collision between French (specialty) and Germany (full capacity) systems derived from the Directive of 1968 and their transactional proposal. In consequence, the adopted scheme followed these rules: legal limitations can be asserted to third parties; those provided in the articles of incorporation cannot be asserted; and, the corporation is linked by these stranger acts not contemplated in the objects clause, except if the corporation could accredit that the third party knew about that unlawful act, or might not ignore it taking into account the circumstances. France integrally adopted the Directive, but Italy added an exception: strange acts to objects clause cannot be asserted to third parties in good faith. Cf. Girón (1976), p. 207. Modern research about the relevance of the directives, in Enriques (2006).

[7] La Villa (1996), pp. 49–50.

[8] Sánchez (1996), pp. 2432–2435.

> Acts done by the organs of the company shall be binding upon it even if those acts are not within the objects of the company unless such acts exceed the powers that the law confers or allows to be conferred on those organs.

The first paragraph postulates a general rule related to the link between corporations, and the acts performed by its directors. This rule was configured from a positive and negative delimitation. Therefore, the act must be part of the board's sphere of duties—although it is not only those legally attributed—but those capable of conferring through the articles of incorporation, even if they are not expressly attributed. Conversely, the objects clause is not a limit to the directors' representative actions because the corporation is bound even if those acts are not listed in the objects clause. Since the Directive just refers to corporations' outside acts involving third parties, it consequently, does not condition the attributed ambit to corporations' inside acts in local legislation referred to in the objects clause.

In turn, the second paragraph provides:

> However, Member States may provide that the company shall not be bound where such acts are outside the objects of the company, if it proves that the third party knew that the act was outside those objects or could not in view of the circumstances have been unaware of it; disclosure of the statutes shall not of itself be sufficient proof thereof.

This provision allows Member States to enact domestic rules in connection with the exclusion of corporate liability because the directors' acts fall under the following conditions: (i) the act goes beyond the objects clause; (ii) the third party had knowledge about the extra limitations in the performance of the act, or under the circumstances, this could not have been ignored. This is a psychological aspect considered the maximum limit in due diligence regarding a third party's knowledge or ignorance. In this respect, national lawmakers were able to establish additional requirements, such as a previous knowledge about the act as it was biased against the corporate interests; (iii) the corporation has to prove the previous circumstances in connection with the transgression of the objects clauses, and its knowledge about it. Consequently, the function of the objects clause as the corporate limit to the directors' representative powers is confined to later legal action of the lawful acts because third parties have nothing to prove in terms of awareness of the act's validity until the corporation takes action.

This provision represents an accommodation between the German doctrine that the validity of a corporate transaction will not be influenced by whether it was carried out within the scope of the company's objects and is dependent only upon the ambit of the representative powers of the organs acting on the company's behalf and the doctrine of *spécialité statutaire* or ultra vires which was accepted subject to certain limitations relating to such matters as an apparent authority and implied ratification in all the five other original Member States. According to the latter doctrine, a transaction was invalid if it did not fall within the objects of the company.[9]

On the other hand, num. 2 provides:

---

[9] Andenas (2009), pp. 42–43. In the opinion of this author, the nature of the compromise contained in art. 9(1) should be fairly obvious from the text of this provision, which stipulates that acts done by the organs of the company shall be binding on it even if these acts are not within the objects of

> The limits on the powers of the organs of the company, arising under the statutes or from a decision of the competent organs, may never be relied on as against third parties, even if they have been disclosed.

This paragraph complements the first paragraph of art. 9.1. In that respect, legal limits are asserted, but voluntaries are not. Therefore, contractual corporate restrictions are just for internal purposes because the director's representative powers are limited only through legal provisions.

Finally, according to paragraph 3:

> If the national law provides that authority to represent a company may, in derogation from the legal rules governing the subject, be conferred by the statutes on a single person or on several persons acting jointly, that law may provide that such a provision in the statutes may be relied on as against third parties on condition that it relates to the general power of representation; the question whether such a provision in the statutes can be relied on as against third parties shall be governed by Article 3.

This article delimits two cardinal aspects concerning the performance and content of the representational powers. In that respect, the Directive contemplates that through the articles of incorporation or because of the decision of the board, the corporation appoints who will be its representative, for example, the president of the board. Then, the law allows attributing the power of representation either in a global or unitary manner, no matter the corporate structure or the contractual regulation in respect to its exercise. Consequently, an individual performance for such an act or transaction and jointly for others is not viable. To conclude, it is expedient to remark that everything presented remains valid nowadays, in the light of the Directive 2009/101/EC art. 10 that exactly reproduced the art. 9 of the First Council Directive 68/151/EEC.

4.2 France

French corporate law has become the cornerstone for other legal systems, and at the same time, the most respected and influential legal body in civil law countries. French corporate law has a blending of legal provisions emerging from the Civil Code and the Commercial Code, without leaving apart special regulations such as the modern SAS. Bearing this introductory context in mind, it is opportune to point out that C.C. art. 1832, defines corporation in the following terms:

> A firm is established by two or several persons which agree by a contract to appropriate property or their industry for a common venture with a view to sharing the benefit or profiting from the saving which may result therefrom.
>
> It may be established, in the cases provided for by statute, through an act of will of one person alone.

---

the company unless such acts exceed the powers which the law confers or allows to be conferred on such organs. As a result, third parties are only protected if the organ acts within the limits of its powers. Ibid.

The members bind themselves to contribute to losses.

It is submitted that such a definition is incomplete because of the lack of another key requisite: the stockholders must have the intention to associate (*affectio societatis*). Reviewing historical backgrounds, French corporate law rests upon two cardinal principles: (i) the corporation is a contract, and (ii) once lawfully incorporated, enjoys legal personality.[10] In that respect, the word 'corporation' has two meanings in the business world: sometimes alluding to the agreement to appropriate money, goods, or labor to execute a commercial activity and share the profits or assume the losses. Another meaning refers to the corporation as the juristic person created for a commercial purpose.

Based on this, the corporate contract requires at least two[11] persons that express their will in a written document containing the agreement to get involved in a business relationship to appropriate property, or their industry for a common venture to share the profits among themselves. Likewise, for any other kind of contract, the corporation must have a licit object, which in this case is the *objects clause*. To the extent that a corporation has been conceived as a contract, the *object* is one of the formal requisites to be in effect. The C.Co. arts. L. 110-1[12] and L. 110-2,[13] providing the type of business activities considered as acts of commerce and therefore the corporate contract must contain at least one of them. However, it is not enough that the act was contemplated by the law as commercial, it must additionally be *licit*. This may seem obvious; nevertheless, it must be kept in mind that, for example, despite smuggling involving a commercial transaction, it is entirely illegal. Also, a fraudulent object produces the same effect as an illicit one. In this respect, when a corporation performs some fraudulent or illicit commercial activity it is not valid to

10 Pothier (1764), pp. 53–58, Malepeyre (1833), pp. 1–3, 23–25, Pardessus (1841), pp. 1–4, Troplong (1843), pp. 9–10, Pic (1908), pp. 247–248, Lyon-Caen (1908), pp. 15–17.

11 However, there are some corporations such as the S.A. that require a minimum of seven stockholders and even could reach millions of them. As pointed out in the first paragraph of C.C. art. 1832, in the case of limited liability corporations, at least two persons are needed to constitute it.

12 C.Co. art. L. 110-1. The law provides that acts of commerce be: (1) All purchases of movable property for the purposes of resale, either as is or after processing and development; (2) All purchases of real property for the purposes of resale, unless the purchaser has acted in order to construct one or more buildings and to sell these en bloc or by individual unit; (3) All operations as intermediary for the purchase, subscription or sale of buildings, businesses or shares of property companies; (4) All companies involved in the rental of movables; (5) All manufacturing, commission, and land or water transport companies; (6) All supply, agency, business office, auction house and public entertainment companies; (7) All exchange, banking, brokering, issuing activity and electronic money management operations and all payment services; (8) All public banking operations; (9) All obligations between dealers, merchants, and bankers; (10) Bills of exchange between all persons.

13 C.Co. art. L. 110-2. The law also deems acts of commerce to be: (1) All construction companies and all purchases, sales, and resales of ships for inland navigation and ships traveling abroad; (2) All sea shipments; (3) All purchases and sales of ship's tackle, apparatus and foodstuffs; (4) All chartering, freighting or bottomry loans; (5) All insurance policies and other contracts relating to maritime trade; (6) All contracts and agreements on crew wages and rents; (7) All engagements of seamen for the service of commercial ships.

ascertain this act as ultra vires, but rather its unlawful quality may drive the firm to its liquidation and the directors to prison.

Thus, it is possible to deem two scenarios: firstly, when the corporation is chartered for a lawful mercantile activity and executes an illegal one. In this case, the corporate contract is valid; however, such a particular act is void not because of ultra vires, but in accordance with general rules in connection with the contract legality of the object. When the objects clause contains an unlawful provision and it is executed, both the corporate contract and the act are void. It is expedient to notice that the objects clause is of such importance, that a substantial modification of it requires a general meeting. Two hypotheses in connection to the change of the objects clause may be submitted: (i) a shift in the *nature* and *manner* of exploitation. When it comes to modify the objects clause in such a way that the nature of the commercial activity suffers a substantial variation, an extraordinary general meeting is required when the objects clause is not flexible enough. On the other hand, (ii) a change in the manner of exploitation has to deal with the substitution of indirect exploitation into direct exploitation. At a first glance, it needs a modification of the objects clause. This assertion leads to admit the possibility to grant a mandate with the previous approbation of the general meeting.[14]

The ultra vires doctrine in French corporate law has plenty of validity due to the principle of specialty (*spécialité statutaire*). This legal device comes from the Conseil d'État that ruled about juristic persons in cases related to gifts destined to public beneficence because of the lack of confidence towards those institutions that could undermine their sovereignty. Latterly, the principle was in effect to private corporate law, with the enacting of Ministerial Ordenance of 1817 that prohibited corporations to perform business activities without a relationship with their objects clause.[15] Indeed, a long time ago some French scholars were reluctant to recognize a *general* patrimonial capacity to moral persons, thus such kinds of entities only have the rights expressly granted by the law. From this perspective, the theory of *spécialité statutaire* confines the existence of the juristic persons to certain acts of civil life, but these limitations are variable in accordance with the nature of the entity. This rationale takes as a starting point the civil nature of the theory of *spécialité statutaire* to derivate in an ondulant and diverse conception of the personality. Conversely to natural persons, the capacity of moral persons subsists by itself with the scope contemplated in the law.[16]

According to the principle of *spécialité statutaire*, corporations can only perform the commercial activities for which they were founded and with strict subjection to the objects clause that delimits the corporation's capacity. In that respect, any act beyond its capacity is a nullity. To avoid incurring in an ultra vires act, by-laws usually include a broad-ranging list of mercantile activities drafting such a clause in prolix terms; however, is it possible to draft a 'universal' objects clause to prevent ultra vires related trials and tribulations? It is convenient to elaborate a list with

[14] Hémard (1974) t. 2, pp. 291–292.

[15] Hauriou (1971), pp. 159–161, Prélot (1978), pp. 616–617, Burdeau (1980), pp. 122–125.

[16] Michoud (1932), pp. 119–121.

countless activities as principal and some others as ancillary to the main object, this corresponds more than a diversification of affairs, but it is recommended to describe a precise list of commercial activities to the end of preventing risky business in hands of neophyte or unscrupulous directors.[17]

On the other hand, in the opinion of Houpin, the meaning of the *object* must be understood as the *cause* that encourages stockholders to associate.[18] Thereby, the goal corresponds to the commercial transactions to execute.[19] As we observe, it looks like there is no difference between the notion of object and cause from this perspective.

Previously we have mentioned capacity as an attribute of corporate personality. In French commercial law, the company's capacity varies depending on the class of corporation. For instance, in the case of the *sociétés en commandite par actions*, some legal provisions prohibit them to engage in certain business activities such as pharmaceutics, money exchange, entities related to gas and electricity public utilities, and so on. However, such restrictions have to deal with the scarce use of these types of companies, more than any consideration about its special nature.[20] Nevertheless, regardless of the type of corporation—except for the SAS—any act executed by a director beyond its powers is void.[21] Conversely to some common law legislations, in

---

[17] Cozian (2009), p. 51.

[18] Houpin (1935), p. 115.

[19] The courts make a distinction between object and cause in the light of corporate law. In re Paris, 13 nov. 1896 (J. S. 1897, US); Alger, 7 nov. 1907 (J. S. 1908, 3766). Compilation by Hémard, 23, 27, 36. Modern authors such as Magnier (2013), pp. 22–24, teach that the objects clause is divided into acts listed in the articles of association, and acts performed by the firm in the market. If there is a contradiction between them the court must determine which one is licit, and let it subsist; on the contrary, it shall impose a sanction for those illegal affairs. However, it is not allowed to compose a 'universal' objects clause where everything has room, but a limited stipulation related to the specific sphere of business in which the company will participate. Thus, the validity of such acts and transactions trusted to directors depends on the manner that the objects clause is structured.

[20] Hémard (1974) t. 2, pp. 1025–1026.

[21] In ancient French corporate law, it was submitted that directors are mandataries, therefore, are granted with powers to manage both affairs and corporate property; nevertheless, they could not sell corporate real state property, either movable goods inside of them, except when they are in peril of being destroyed. Vid. Pothier (1764), pp. 60–61. When the corporation's directors were stockholders, they had the broadest powers to manage all of the business. In that respect, they could engage in any kind of act or transaction; but when it comes to the sale of real state property, directors will need stockholders' consent. See, Malepeyre (1833), pp. 53–55. In the case of joint-stock companies, this author notes that the power to sell is not an act of administration, but of disposition, in consequence, it is the general meeting that must approve it. Op. cit., pp. 237–239. Nowadays as recognized by courts, the directors have the power to sell property, even if it is the only one owned by the corporation. In re Cass. 3ᵉ Civ. 18, déc. 2001.

See, Berr (1961) for detailed analysis of the representation mechanism and its relationship to corporate structure and inside the organization. Furthermore, there is a study of the cooperation/subordination link between the corporations' "organs". On the other hand, this monograph rememorizes the distinction between representatives' powers and managerial activities.

French corporate law, it is mandatory to have both the memorandum and the articles of association,[22] in fact, the C.Co. art. L210-7, second paragraph, provides:

> If the memorandum and articles of association do not contain all the statements required by law and the regulations or if a formality laid down by these for the formation of the company has been omitted or not accomplished in due form, any interested party shall be entitled to apply to a court for an order to be made that the formation must be regularized or a fine imposed.

An interesting provision is contained in the second paragraph of art. L210-6:

> Persons who have acted in the name of a company in formation before it has acquired enjoyment of legal personality shall be held jointly and indefinitely liable for the acts thus accomplished unless the company, after having been formed and registered in due form, takes over its obligations thus entered into. These obligations shall then be deemed to have been entered into from the start by the company.

In general partnership corporations (*société en nom collectif*) art. L221-4 provides:

> In dealings between partners and in the absence of limitation of their powers by the memorandum and articles of association, the manager may perform all acts of management in the interests of the partnership. In the event of there being more than one manager, each shall hold separately the powers specified in the preceding subparagraph, except that each shall have the right to object to any transaction prior to its conclusion.

In the same way art. L221-5 provides that in general partnership corporations in dealings with third parties, the manager shall bind the partnership by acts within the purpose of the company. Clauses of the memorandum and articles of association limiting the powers of the managers resulting from this article shall be ineffective against third parties.

Demogue points out that when the publicity given to the by-laws of the association easily permits third persons to obtain knowledge that a certain act cannot be undertaken in the name of the association by its managers, if legislation, as in France, has not provided for acts ultra vires committed by the directors, we may posit the following principle: third persons who deal with the association know, or ought to know, that the by-laws forbid a certain act. If they are ignorant, it is their fault. Consequently, when a clause has been duly published limiting the powers of the directors, it may be invoked against third persons. This solution, which by a middle course reconciles the security of the company with that of third persons, appears to us possible of adoption in all countries where the question has not been settled by legislation.[23] This is the solution adopted in France by the *Cour de Cassation* in a case where the corporate by-laws forbade the associates to issue notes or to sign any drafts obligating the company, even with the concurrence of other associates and

---

[22] C.C. art. 1835: "The memorandum and the articles of association must be drawn up in writing. They shall determine, in addition to the contributions of each member, the form, *objects*, name, duration, registered place of business, capital of the firm, and its rules of functioning" (italics supplied).

[23] Demogue (1922), pp. 631–632.

under penalty of being null and void as against third parties. The *Cour de Cassation* said:

> It is within the power of the contracting parties to limit in their collective or individual interest the powers of the directors of the company by forbidding them to undertake certain predetermined acts. This obligatory prohibition laid upon the associates may likewise be set up against third persons by reason of the publicity which the articles of association have received.[24]

If, on the contrary, publicity has not taken place, Professor Demogue claims that the clause cannot be set up against third persons. This also the *Cour de Cassation* has decided when confronted with a formal provision of articles of association according to which the associates could not sign notes for the purchase of merchandise "when it was not duly established that this clause was included in the publication which alone could render it possible to set it up against third persons".[25] In all these cases in which the mere examination of the contract proposed to third persons makes it possible in the light of the by-laws to determine whether the contract is valid, it is the fact of publicity, or non-publicity, of the articles that determine the issue against or in favor of third persons.

Taking into account the directors' liability, art. L221-6 states that decisions exceeding the powers accorded to the managers shall be taken by unanimous agreement of the partners. However, the memorandum and articles of association may specify that certain decisions shall be taken by a specified majority.

By Decree 69-1.176, French legislators reformed corporate law, warning that any act beyond the objects clause cannot be asserted to third parties in good faith. In this case, the corporation must evidence that such a third party had prior knowledge about the act was performed outside the objects clause, or it shall not be ignored under the circumstances.

On the other hand, genuine legislative innovation in French corporate law emerged in 1994, with the enactment of Law 94-1 by which the SAS[26] was created. In fact, a certain writer said that it was corporate law's "big-bang". As a result of the rigidity of current corporate law legislation, entrepreneurs required a flexible tool that allows them to self-determinate the crucial aspects of business life, and it was then when the SAS came out to satisfy these necessities. The main structural characteristic of the SAS is the prevalence of contract freedom; therefore, the majority of legal provisions may be derogated by stockholder will throughout the corporate contract stipulations. This is a very special type of simplified joint-stock company that may be established by only *one* person (physical or juristic); therefore, the paradigm of the corporation as a "contract" has been replaced for the corporation as a creation of a unilateral "act" in the case of just one associate. When the SAS consists of one person only, the single member shall exercise all of the powers conferred to the members when collective decision-making is needed. Likewise, the powers of the board or its president shall

[24] Chambre Civil, Dec. 22, 1874, Dalloz, 1875, I, 255.

[25] Chambre des Requetes, August 16, 1875, Dalloz, 1876, I, 422.

[26] Merle (2005), pp. 709–723, Gavalda (2009), pp. 409–417, Ripert (2009), pp. 116–138, 701–710.

be exercised by the president of the SAS or by those directors that the incorporation act appoints for this purpose.[27]

On the contrary to any other class of French corporation, the SAS could have an indeterminate objects clause, or even better, a "generic" objects clause that will allow it to enter into any kind of legal activity; in that respect, except if it is limited to certain kind of commercial activities, it should be rare that a SAS could fall in an ultra vires act. For the purpose of this writing, the main provision in connection with the ultra vires doctrine is the C.Co. art. L. 227-6:

> The company is represented in its dealings with third parties by a president appointed as prescribed in the constitution. The president is invested with the most extensive powers to act on behalf of the company in all circumstances, within the limits of the corporate objects.
>
> In its dealings with third parties, the company is bound even by acts of the president that do not come within the purview of the company's corporate objects, unless it can prove that the third party knew that a specific action was outside those objects or, given the circumstances, could not have been ignorant of that fact, and mere publication of the constitution does not suffice to constitute such proof.
>
> The constitution may stipulate the circumstances in which one or more persons other than the president, having the title of managing director or deputy managing director, may exercise the powers conferred on the president by the present Article.
>
> Provisions in the constitution which limit the president's powers cannot be raised against third parties.

As we notice, this provision encompasses some directions of the Directive 68/151/CEE, common law provisions in connection with the UK CA 1985, and the USA MBCA. In the frame of this contract freedom, the director could be freely appointed by the general meeting and granted the broadest powers to perform any kind of affair in the best interest of the company. However, even in the world of SAS, the law lays out that directors' powers should be framed in the objects clause, i.e., it recognizes that even in a predominantly contractual environment, the company's capacity is limited to the acts of commerce described in the articles of incorporation.

Finally, the second paragraph contains the most relevant provision in connection with ultra vires doctrine, contemplating the corporate responsibility when the president engages in a business transaction outside of the corporate capacity, except if

[27] Gierke regarded one-man companies with disfavor. He saw in them abuse of legal conceptions and considered that there is no doubt that abuses occur. Thus, when company A buys up all the shares of company B in order that it may cloak, under the name of B, any dealings which are to be concealed from its shareholders. Or again, when companies are created with the sole purpose of masking the real actor. In these cases, legal personality acts as a smoke-screen. Another case of abuse occurs fairly frequently on the Continent. The articles of a company sometimes provide that a shareholder holding more than, e.g., five shares have, on a poll, only five votes. Mr. A has 1.000 shares, and in order to obtain 1.000 votes, he founds 199 private companies, in conjunction with Mr. Dummy—a Dr. Jekyll who creates a whole army of Mr. Hyde. In each of these companies, Mr. A and Mr. Dummy are the only members and to each company Mr. A transfers 5 of his shares, retaining 5 for himself. The practice of founding one-man companies in order to avoid income tax or super-tax should also count among the abuses. Abuses, then, do exist, and the Courts of all countries might deal with them more severely than is actually done. Cf. Wolff (1938), pp. 502–503.

it can be evidenced that the third party was cognizant about the want of capacity because such act was not contemplated in the objects clause.

4.3 Germany

Prior to address the ultra vires doctrine in Germany, it is expedient to take a look at the various forms of business organizations in such a country. Professor Schulz deliveries a brief overview of the most important non-corporate and hybrid forms of business organizations available under German law. In doing so, he explains that "German business law provides for various types of business organization such as corporations, partnerships and associations. The most important types of corporations are the GmbH and the AG. There are three types of partnership, the BGB Gesellschaf (civil law partnership), the oHG (general commercial partnership) and the KG (limited commercial partnership). Although corporations, and in particular the GmbH, are quite popular, there may also be reasons to choose a partnership as the legal vehicle for conducting business, e.g. partners have a greater flexibility in management issues and in regards to the dissolution of the partnership. Moreover, in a partnership there are fewer publication requirements and a higher level of confidentiality. For these reasons partnerships are often selected as the business vehicle for small entities or family-owned enterprises.

(i) Sole Proprietorship (einzelkaufmännisches Unternehmen). This business form is typically used by small enterprises. Since it is the easiest way to start and run a business, it is one of the most prevalent forms of small business organizations for entrepreneurs in Germany. A sole proprietorship is an unincorporated business, owned by a single person and operated in her/his name or under a trade name. The sole proprietorship is not a legal entity. Thus, it cannot have any rights and obligations of its own, nor can it sue or be sued in court. Instead, it is the owner (Einzelkaufmann) who holds all the rights and who is fully liable for all business debts and obligations. Depending on its size and range of activities, the sole proprietorship has to be registered with the Commercial Register. If the sole proprietor is not legally obliged to register, she/he may still choose to do so voluntarily. However, in both cases (mandatory and voluntary registration), the sole proprietor—being a 'merchant' according to the definition of German commercial law—has to comply with many of the HGB's regulations.

(ii) Civil Law Partnership (GbR). In contrast to the AG and GmbH, the civil law partnership (Gesellschaft bürgerlichen Rechts, GbR or BGB-Gesellschaft) is an association of two or more persons without corporate organization. The GbR does not have the status of a corporation as a separate legal entity. The GbR is established by setting up a partnership agreement between at least two partners wishing to pursue any legal purpose. However, if the partners intend to pursue a commercial business, this partnership will be treated as a general commercial partnership (oHG) or as a limited commercial partnership (KG).

(iii) Civil Law Partnership (GbR). In contrast to the AG and GmbH, the civil law partnership (Gesellschaft bürgerlichen Rechts, GbR or BGB-Gesellschaft) is an as-sociation of two or more persons without corporate organization. The GbR does not have the status of a corporation as a separate legal entity. The GbR is established by setting up a partnership agreement between at least two partners wishing to pursue any legal purpose. However, if the partners intend to pursue a commercial business, this partnership will be treated as a general commercial partnership (oHG) or as a limited commercial partnership (KG).

The GbR is managed and represented jointly by all partners, unless the partnership agreement provides otherwise. The assets of the partnership belong to its partners jointly. All partners are jointly and severally liable for the firm's debts and obligations. Such liability may be limited to the partnership assets only by agreement with the third party creditor or by restrictions set out in the partnership agreement and made known to the third party creditor. Because of its flexibility, the GbR is used for a great variety of business purposes.

Beginning in 2001, the Bundesgerichtshof fundamentally changed the traditional statutory regime for the GbR in several landmark decisions by treating this company form in a way similar to that of a general commercial partnership.

- In its decision of 29 January 2001 , the BGH acknowledged the capacity of a GbR to sue and be sued in private proceedings. Furthermore, the court applied the liability rules for partners of German commercial partnerships (oHG, KG) to partners of a private law partnership. The extension of these liability rules means that, for claims against that partnership, creditors may hold partners of a private law partnership personally liable.
- With its decision of 24 February 2002, the BGH further extended the liability of the civil law partnership by ruling that damages caused by the managing directors have to be compensated by the civil law partnership. The court emphasized that partners of a private law partnership are personally and jointly liable for the liabilities of that partnership.
- In another landmark decision of 7 April 2003 , the BGH held that a new partner of a private law partnership may be held liable for obligations that arose even before she/he joined the private law partnership. With this decision, the Court thus further expanded the personal liability of partners of a private law partnership by analogizing them to partners of a commercial law partnership. In essence, the Bundesgerichtshof has treated the private law partnership as a legal entity quite similar to the general commercial partnership (described below) and, in effect, thus transformed the GbR into a legal entity that now largely approximates the general commercial partnership.

(iv) General Commercial Partnership (oHG). The general commercial partnership (offene Handelsgesellschaft, oHG) is a partnership established by two or more per-sons for the purpose of operating a commercial business within the meaning of the Commercial Code (vollkaufmännisches Handelsgewerbe) under a company name, provided that all partners are fully liable for the partnership's debts and obligations. It is formed by agreement between the partners, which may be concluded even by conduct. After that, the oHG must be registered in the Commercial Register. In contrast to the GbR, the oHG has a company name under which it may acquire rights of its own, incur obligations and sue or be sued in court (see section 124 HGB). Although the oHG has a status similar to that of a corporation regarding its dealings with third parties, significant differences to corporations do remain. For instance, the assets of the oHG belong to all partners jointly and the partners are jointly and severally liable for the oHG's debts and obligations. Each partner is individually entitled to manage and represent the partnership, unless the partnership agreement provides otherwise by consent of all partners. The oHG is a business form typically used by a small number of partners who personally rely on each other and wish to commit all their assets to a joint undertaking. However, the overall importance of the oHG has significantly decreased and other company forms (not demanding the personal liability of its members) have become more popular. As of 1 January 2010 in Germany 27, 422 oHGs were registered.

(v) Limited Commercial Partnership (KG). The limited commercial partnership (Kommanditgesellschaft, KG) is a general partnership similar to the oHG, in that it is also a partnership established for the purpose of operating a commercial business. In contrast to the oHG, however, the KG has two kinds of partners. There are one or more general partners (persönlich haftende Gesellschafter or Komplementäre) with unlimited personal liability (identical to a partner in an oHG). These partners with personal liability manage and represent the limited commercial partnership. On the other hand, there are one or more 'limited partners' (Kommanditisten) whose per-sonal liability is limited to the amount of a fixed capital contribution to be paid to the partnership. The amount of this capital contribution is registered in the Commer-cial Register (Handelsregister) and, to the extent it has been paid into the limited commercial partnership and has not been repaid, the limited partner is discharged from personal liability. The limited partners are excluded from the management and representation of the partnership, unless the partnership agreement provides otherwise.

The KG is frequently used for family-owned enterprises. Quite often it has also been used to bring together capital from investors for particular ventures. The KG is particularly popular in a form in which the sole general partner is a corporation, typically, a GmbH. As of 1 January 2010 there were 236.554 limited commercial partnerships registered in Germany. (See Kornblum 2010, p. 740).

(vi) Hybrid Commercial Limited Partnership (GmbH & Co. KG). A frequently used combination of the limited commercial partnership and the corporation is that of a KG, in which the only general partner is a GmbH (so-called GmbH & Co. KG). By allowing the KG to have corporations such as the GmbH as a partner with full personal liability (so-called Komplementär), personal liability can be avoided in a legally permissible way since, in principle, only the GmbH (and not its shareholders) will be liable vis-à-vis the creditors of the KG. The attractiveness of the GmbH & Co. KG results from the fact that it combines the advantages of a partnership (tax benefits) with those of a corporation (limitation of liability), which may outweigh the disadvantages resulting from a somewhat complex corporate structure.

(vii) Partnership Limited by Shares (KGaA). The partnership limited by shares (Kommanditgesellschaft auf Aktien, KGaA) is another hybrid business form combining elements of a limited commercial partnership with those of a stock corporation. Partnership law is applicable for those partners with personal liability whereas the KGaA and the partners with limited liability (Kommanditaktionäre) are subject to the German Stock Corporation Act (Sec. 278, paras. 2 and 3 AktG). Due to its relative complexity the KGaA is not common in German legal practice: As of 1 June 2010 only 225 partnerships limited by shares were in existence.

(viii) Silent Partnership (stille Gesellschaft). The silent partnership (stille Gesellschaft) is a partnership as set forth in section 705 BGB but is designed as an internal legal relationship characterized by someone participating in the commercial trade of another person with a capital contribution which will then be transferred to the assets of the business partner. For this purpose a contract between the proprietor of the commercial trade and the so-called 'silent' participant is mandatory. Only the proprietor will enter into transactions and will be liable for and entitled from the business transactions. The silent partner is only liable for her/his capital contribution towards her/his partner. In practice, a silent partnership may be chosen for tax reasons or because of confidentiality interests of the investor (e.g. in a family business).

(ix) Registered Cooperative (eingetragene Genossenschaft). The registered cooperative (eingetragene Genossenschaft, eG) is an association with an unlimited number of members whose purpose is to promote the goals of its members—this can be a commercial goal as well as for a social or cultural purpose. This type of business association originated in the nineteenth century and was a popular vehicle especially for craftsmen and farmers. But even today, the eG is quite common in some business sectors (e.g. retail and banking), and there are approximately 7.000 registered cooperatives with nearly twenty million members . The eG is defined as a separate legal entity and can acquire rights and assume liabilities; it may acquire ownership and other real property rights, and it can sue and can be sued.[28]

[28] Schulz et al. (2012)

At an early stage of the modern treatment of the ultra vires doctrine, a monograph about it was written by Schlink (1935) from a German civil law overview, and nowadays a college thesis authored by Lettmaier (2006). As recounted recently by Guinnane,[29] at the onset of the 19th century, German law reflected a deep French influence especially extended to commercial law matters. However, German company law diverged significantly from that in other industrial countries, including France. Some of that divergence reflects a different approach to company law, and some reflect the importance of enterprise forms more important in Germany than elsewhere.

For example, in the joint-stock company according to original HGB §182(2) the memorandum of association should set forth the *objects* of the undertaking. At the time, the objects were understood as synonymous with their purpose. Nevertheless, the special means chosen in every case to reach the company's general purpose is their object that should be listed in the memorandum of association. In other words, the object of the undertaking is the means to get profits, i.e., the branch of commercial operations. Taking into account such provision, some critics arose regarding the compulsory need to include the objects in the memorandum of association as explained previously. On one hand, it is not necessary to confine it in a detailed fashion because it is enough to point out a broad expression such as "any kind of business". After all, the law does not make it mandatory to include a detailed roster of commercial activities. On the other hand, taking into account that joint-stock companies have special regulations that make it mandatory to list commercial activities to protect third parties, not leaving it to the corporate organs to determine the objects and declare a branch of business in which the corporation will trade.[30]

Until 1900 and the introduction of the all-German BGB, Prussia's Rhineland province retained the French Civil Code for civil law matters. In 1861, Prussia, along with nearly all-German states, adopted the ADHGB, creating legal uniformity for commercial law. The North German Confederation and later Reich adopted the ADHGB, as well. In 1900, a unified Germany adopted its new Civil Code (BGB), and at the same time put into force a new Commercial Code (HGB) completed in 1897. The 1897 HGB integrated the new corporate law, along with some small reforms into the Reich's business code.

Most German governments strictly limited access to the corporate form until 1870. After 1884, legislation intended to protect shareholders and creditors made the corporation less attractive than its counterpart in the UK, USA, and other industrial

[29] Guinnane (2018), pp. 170–172. An oddity of the 1965 reform was the near-abolishment of freedom of contract with respect to the articles of association. Without any real discussion and without probing the issue properly, the legislator held it to be an accepted principle of German corporate law tradition that in the articles of association, any deviation from the AktG was forbidden if not expressly permitted in the AktG. See, Kuntz (2018), pp. 228–229. It is been discussed the development of German corporate law by focusing on the French *Code de Commerce* of 1807, which is identified as the first true general corporate law, allowing for incorporation by way of a more normative and permissive system of concession by the state and with limited liability. The historical account concentrates on the use of the French and other comparative law precedents as the basis for the first German corporate laws of the early to mid-nineteenth century. Vid. Muchlinski (2013), p. 343.

[30] Fischer (1934), pp. 121–124.

countries. Following the French practice, German entrepreneurs organized 'share partnerships', a form of limited partnership with tradable shares representing limited partnership interests. This form offered some of the corporate advantages but did not (in certain times and places) require state permission. Efforts to regulate the shared partnership influenced the treatment of corporations.

Another corporation-like enterprise form, the bG, reflected older practices for mines. The bG remained popular for mines until the liberalization of corporation laws, and also underlies the GmbH, a limited liability form well suited to small and medium-sized enterprises (SMEs). The GmbH's introduction in 1892 reflected perceived limitations in corporate law.

Indeed, conversely to other civil law countries such as Colombia or France, as Schlüter teaches, German company law provisions appear disseminated all over their legal system dealing with each class of corporation, and in some cases, specific topics (e.g., mergers or accounting). Taking into account this legal context, there is almost no applicable general rule for every kind of firm.[31] Therefore, we will focus on the two main German corporation types: the AG regulated by AktG law, and the GmbH regulated by the GmbHG law.[32] Since the time of its original adoption in 1892, the GmbH law has not undergone any material change. The only significant subsequent statutes which have materially affected the operation and management of a GmbH, have been the so-called "co-determination laws" adopted in a series commencing in 1951 and ending with the adoption of the most recent statute in 1976, and the so-called "publicity law". These statutes essentially affected only the internal management structure of the GmbH and certain matters of financial disclosure but did not affect other aspects of its organization and operation.

German corporate legislation is a product of the views of legal technicians as to the needs of the business world, indirectly influenced by ideology. The economic miracle took place under the aegis of a corporation law which, enacted in 1937, was tainted here and there by National Socialist phraseology and, less frequently, by its rather vague economic philosophy. In general, the 1937 law was felt to have proved itself in its twenty-eight years of crisis-ridden life, but there were pressures for changes in some aspects. Finally, after many years of study and debate, the corporation law reform bill was passed in 1965. It borrowed certain institutions from the USA, particularly in the financial and accounting area, and in the arrangements for shareholder voting, and it corrected various minor failings but it left the basic structure of the 1937 Act untouched.[33]

Historically, the German legal system has considered all kinds of juristic persons with a full capacity to perform any act likewise flesh and bone people.[34] In that respect, the legislators equated personality to capacity; therefore, assuming that

[31] Schlüter (1991), pp. 277–286.

[32] Ercklentz (1981), p. 646.

[33] Vagts (1966), pp. 30–31.

[34] This point of view has led to assert that ultra vires doctrine does not have room in Germany. Cf. Serick (1958), pp. 86, 90. Meanwhile, others conceive its validity but with a limited scope. Vid. Gierke (1957), p. 261. In fact, after 1850, corporations with unspecified objects became more numerous. See, Muchlinski (2013), p. 347. Therefore, with such broad capacity, it is inconceivable

corporations interact in the business world through organs and not by representatives, thus the organs' acts are the corporations' acts regardless of what kind they are.

One of the most influential legal institutions in German private law is the theory of representation. According to BGB §164, it is possible to attribute an act to the undertaking under two assumptions: firstly, the individual must have acted in the name of the titular of the right—e.g., the corporation, and secondly, should have acted having the power of representation. Schmidt criticizes the theory of "organic representation" because if it is so, the corporation would act for itself and no representation shall be needed. In that respect, to verify whether an act can be ascribed to the corporation (AktG §78; GmbHG §35), it is necessary to evidence if the act is executed in the name of the corporation and if the individual had the power of representation.[35]

In turn, a distinction must be made between corporate purpose (*Zweck*) and the corporate object (*Gegenstand*). When the *material* activity determines the commercial or industrial scope of the business, we are within the scenario of the object. Conversely, the corporate purpose has to deal with the goal that shareholders had in mind when founding a specific type of corporation, fulfilling the legal requirements. Despite such a theory that segregates material and legal activities, we are doubtful about this differentiation because the corporate purpose could be contained in the object itself.

Schuster explains that "a corporation without the capacity for acts-in-the-law is as inconceivable as a corporation without any capacity for rights, but like the capacity for rights, the disposing capacity may be restricted by the constitution of the corporation. A corporation must of necessity act through one or more persons appointed as its primary agents; these primary agents must be distinguished from agents appointed by the primary agents, whose powers may be as varied as the powers of the agents of natural persons, but the primary agents must always have certain express or implied powers of acting on behalf of the corporation whom they represent. In English law, such powers are not as a rule defined by any general rules but vary according to the constitution of the particular corporation; in Germany, on the other hand, certain fixed rules are laid down as to the powers of the primary agents of each class of corporations regulated by general law. Thus it frequently happens in the case of companies formed under the British Companies Acts that the powers of the directors

that an act or transaction could go beyond the scope of their capacity (ultra vires). In the case of the GmbH, the 1892 GmbHG law, provided that the objects clause must be described in the articles of incorporation; however, it is not mandatory to confine it in a rigorous and detailed fashion, but just to draw a general formula, from which any person could easily evidence the nature of business. See, Feine (1930), pp. 40–41.

[35] Schmidt (1997), pp. 475–479. Since the ancient German commercial law (ADHGB) has existed the *Prokura* as a power of representation, which mitigates the risk associated with acts performed by legal representatives contradicting the instructions given by the principal in a major way. In accordance with HGB §49, the *Prokura* contains a power of representation for any kind of acts related to the commercial activity, and cannot be confined to specific acts, or limited in time or space (§49). However, the *Prokura* must be related to the objects clause because, to the contrary, any amendment of the objects clause exceeds the power of representation of the *Prokurist*. Cf. Op. cit. p. 480, et seq.

do not go as far as the powers of the company and that acts, though intra vires of the company, are invalid on the ground that they are ultra vires of the directors, and ought therefore to have been confirmed by a general meeting".[36]

According to Professor Schuster "in the case of trading corporations formed under German Imperial law, this would be impossible, as the law confers general powers on the directors of such undertakings to act on behalf of the company, and it is impossible to restrict such general powers in any way to affect third parties".[37] In the case of firms incorporated under the provisions of the BGB (§26, §64, and §70), restrictions affecting third parties may be imposed upon the powers of directors subject to compliance with the prescribed rules as to registration, but in the absence of such registered restrictions, the company directors are entitled to exercise all the powers of the corporation.

Under this legal context, it is appropriate to point out that ultra vires doctrine has no room in German company law. According to early UK and USA law, any transaction entered into by an incorporated company, for any object not included in the objects mentioned in the memorandum of association, was void on the ground of being ultra vires of the corporation. In Germany, no transaction entered into by one of the primary agents of a corporation formed under the HGB (§59 and §60), or the Limited Partnership Act (§61), is invalid on the grounds that it is outside of the scope of the usual corporate business, or of the objects for which the corporation was created. If an English company established for trading, undertook the construction of a bridge, or a flying machine, the contract would be invalid, but a similar contract entered into on behalf of a similar German company by one of its primary agents would be binding on the company if otherwise in order.

Broad-ranging powers assigned to corporate directors have a sociological background. Vagts claims that German executives tend to be more independent, self-willed, and bent upon success in strictly business terms, and less dependent on their colleagues' approval of their public-spiritedness. In this way German managements are less remote from the epoch of individual or family ownership or control and that their experiences with war and inflation have left them with a feeling that it is far more urgent to perform their economic tasks than to scatter their energies on peripheral function.[38]

In such a broad frame of reference as described and because corporate law provisions were at first time supplementary, the firm's founders illegally took advantage of it at the expense of shareholders and creditors to execute fraudulent financial operations. Noticing this anomalous situation both lawmakers and judges were progressively introducing mandatory rules to avoid such kind of unlawful conduct. Taking into account that AG was generally used to those ends, back in 1965 the Stock

[36] Schuster (1907), p. 36.

[37] Schuster (1907), p. 36. Accordingly to the following legislation: HGB 231–235; Limited Partnership Act (1892, revised 1898) ss. 35–37; Act relating to Cooperative Societies (1889, revised 1898) ss. 24, 27; Private Insurance Act (1901) s. 34.

[38] Vagts (1966), p. 43.

Corporation Act ruled that their provisions were mandatory except where expressly permitted.[39]

The AG is the form used mainly by large companies whose shares are publicly held and which are traded on a stock exchange. As mentioned above, while the history of the stock corporation dates back to the middle of the 18th century, its codification began in the mid-19th century. Incorporation without special dispensation from the state became available in 1870. The stock corporation law was taken out of the general Commercial Code and separately codified in 1937. The current law, which dates from 1965, is based on the 1937 law but also includes many significant changes and refinements. The act has been amended frequently since its enactment, but none of them has to deal with the ultra vires doctrine. However, it is important to warn that articles of incorporation must specify the corporate purpose. This statement limits management authority but not its power to act; management may bind the corporation outside the scope of the stated purpose but may find itself liable for damages suffered by the corporation from such acts.[40]

According to AktG §23(1) the by-laws must be established by way of being recorded by a notary. Authorized representatives may act only if they have a power of attorney certified by a notary. In turn, par. (3)2, provides that the by-laws must determine the purpose of the enterprise; specifically, industrial and trade enterprises are to provide details regarding the nature of the products and goods that are to be manufactured and traded.

On the other hand, AktG §82 in connection with restrictions on the power to represent the company and to manage its affairs provides:

(1) It is not possible to restrict the power of representation of the management board.

(2) In their relationship to the company, the members of the management board are under obligation to comply with the restrictions on the authority to manage the affairs of the company that have been established, in the context of creating the regulations governing the stock corporation, in the by-laws, by the supervisory board, the general meeting, as well as by the rules of procedure of the management board and of the supervisory board.

With the purpose of protecting shareholder rights from abusive practices arising from the management board, the principles related to mandate should be applied to num. (1). In this respect, the mandatary (board) must agree to carry out the transactions entrusted by those mandating (shareholders) for their benefit, and strictly in accordance with the powers given to them. Conversely, the opposite thesis holds that market interests are upon individual ones. Therefore, the representational power of the board must not be restricted, and only in cases of abuse are shareholders encouraged to file a suit against board members for damages.

To resolve the conflict of interests between shareholder protection and commercial business activities, the German model has proposed the principle of "traffic

---

39 Currently, AktG §23(5) provides: "The by-laws may deviate from the regulations of the present Act only where this has been expressly permitted. Supplementing the by-laws by additional determinations is permissible unless the present Act provides conclusively for the matter".

40 Schneider (1996), pp. 3, 5.

protection". Thus, the company is run by everyone under the statutory power of representation. Restrictions permitted on the powers of the organs only affect legal requirements in the internal relations (management authority) and leave the legal skills in external relations (power of representation).

In turn, according to GmbHG §1: "A limited liability company may be formed by one person or several persons pursuant to the provisions of this Act for any purpose permitted by law". Conversely to AktG, the GmbHG did not define such a class of corporation. However, since 1884 legislators conceived the GmbH as a hybrid between the joint-stock company and the limited partnership. Indeed, there were two defined ideological models regarding it. The first group considered the GmbH as a limited partnership but with a narrow scope of liability, and the second group, as a "soft" stock company with plenty of dispositive provisions, eliminating the rigid foundation rules and setting accessory obligations. Finally, this type of corporation was born in 1892, and since then until the present time few changes have been made.[41] As we observe, taking into account GmbHG §1 it is hard to consider that a company organized as GmbH could incur in an ultra vires act.

Due to such versatility, the GmbH is a device to carry out any legitimate objectives with the protection of limited liability. It can be utilized to serve small companies as well as enterprises with a multi-million dollar capital, one-man proprietorships, and partnerships, as well as companies open to amplifying membership. It is well suited to provide a means of formalizing subsidiaries, holding companies, and joint ventures, and has been used to form pools, combines, and cartels. Its objective need not be an activity for gain. Even a judicial settlement may be organized as a GmbH. Private parties using the GmbH find it an exceedingly pliable device because of the freedom of contract they enjoy with respect to the charter. The legislative technique for giving the members of a GmbH this autonomy is the use of "dispositive norms", i.e., statutory rules that apply only in the absence of specific mandatory stipulations.[42]

Now, GmbHG §37 related to restrictions on the power of representation lays out:

(1) The directors shall be obligated vis-à-vis the company to observe those restrictions which have been set out in the articles of association as regards the extent of their power to represent the company or, unless otherwise provided therein, by resolutions passed by the shareholders.

(2) A restriction of the directors' power to represent the company shall have no legal effect with respect to third persons. This shall, in particular, apply to those cases in which the representation is restricted to certain business or types of business only or only under certain circumstances or for a certain period of time or in specific places, or where the consent of the shareholders or a company organ is required for the conduct of specific business.

Usually, any transaction entered into by the managers acting for the GmbH in proper form is binding on the company. This is true even when the managerial action is in disregard of express directives issued by the quota holders or restrictions contained in the charter. Although such restrictions require the managers to act accordingly, they

[41] Ulmer (1998), pp. 27–31.

[42] De Vries (1964), pp. 867–868.

do not affect their power to bind the company. However, under certain circumstances, a third party may be estopped from relying on the validity of a transaction entered into by the manager in disregard of his duties.[43]

4.4 Italy

Italian legislation does not contemplate an ad hoc rule about the juristic capacity of collective entities. In that respect, the law does not specify if they have full capacity as in the German system, or are confined to a specific purpose in the likeness of the common law system. However, they should have a full capacity as flesh and bone individuals, of course with the obvious limitations.[44] A distinction must be made between the company's will and the expression of such will with regards to third parties. In that respect, it is possible that both do not concur with the same individuals. Thus, the objects clause plays a key role as the limit to company capacity, or as a limit to the general meeting, and it is relevant to determining the liability of directors. Therefore, the ultra vires doctrine deals with the former, and such lack of capacity is abuse as opposed to an excess of director power. Conversely, when the directors perform an act exceeding their powers the company, it cannot be linked to it.[45]

The corporation is a juristic mechanism to execute business collectively. In this way, the firm's goals aim to perform an economic activity with a speculative objective. Thus, the legal concept of a company has a double dimension from their business activity to its organizational structure. At this point, it is opportune to mention that the Italian concept of the company as a "plurilateral" contract, dominates the academic opinion among both Latin American and European corporate law scholars.[46]

---

43 De Vries (1964), p. 879. This author points out that restrictions may result from various sources, such as express charter provisions, quota-holders' resolutions, directives of the supervisory board, employment agreements, and internal rules. An example of such a restriction is the corporate purpose. Likewise other restrictions, it does not limit a manager's power to act as a legal representative of the corporation. As a result, German corporate law has no doctrine of ultra vires. In re Reichsgericht (I. Zivilsenat), Nov. 19, 1926, 115 R.G.Z. 246, in which the court held that action by the board of an AG to acquire quotas in an independent GmbH was valid although the resulting combination did not agree with corporate purposes. Vid. op. cit., footnote 94. In the GmbH, it is mandatory to appoint a director by the general meeting in accordance with §46.5. Directors are granted unlimited powers of representation; in consequence, such powers cannot be supplanted or postponed by the general meeting. In turn, the fulfillment of corporate agreements related to management outside the scope of the firm is only binding to the directors. Cf. Ulmer (1996), pp. 68–70.

44 Breccia (1995), pp. 277–279.

45 Ascarelli (1951), pp. 50–51; 112.

46 A special mention to Tullio Ascarelli, El Contrato Plurilateral, México (1949). This essay was a pioneer in discussing the contractual relationship between more than two parts, in opposition to the traditional concept of unilateral and bilateral contracts. Extensive research regarding the corporate contract and the associative contract in Italy and comparative with Germany and France, in Ferro (2001), 2–24. It is expedient to bear in mind a distinction between *objects clause* and the *object of the company*. The latter has to deal with the economic activity for which performance the corporation

In accordance with C.C. art. 2247, through a corporate contract, two or more persons confer goods or services for the joint exercise of economic activities to divide the profits among themselves. As an essential requisite of the corporate contract from an *objective* point of view, this specific economic activity becomes the objects clause that allows making a distinction between the commercial companies and another kind of association. On the other hand, from a *subjective* perspective, the objects clause must be jointly executed by all corporators, of course, according to the type of company, the management will be delegated in some organs as the board of directors.[47]

As in Germany, in Italy, there are two main types of companies in which the capital is divided by shares (SPA) and by quotas (SRL). We will discuss those types of business entities.

Italian company law recognizes corporate purpose as a key element of the corporate contract that gives birth to the firm. The corporate purpose has to deal with those commercial activities for which the firm was founded, and likewise any other kind of contract, such an object must be determinate. To validate if the director executed an act beyond their powers or the company's capacity (ultra vires), the corporate contract must be interpreted as a whole and taking into account the initial intentions of the founding associates. The company's purpose may be confined to only one type of business or a lot of them.[48]

As a transversal requisite to any type of company, the C.C. art. 2295, num. 5, lays out that articles of association must indicate the objects clause; however, this provision does not prescribe the manner in which commercial or industrial activities should be described.[49] Taking into account that companies have a contractual origin, a remission must be done to art. 1346, ibid. that provides the law of obligations as a general principle: "The object of the contract must be possible, licit, determinate or determinable". In this case, the objects clause must be understood as the company's economic activity. Such an indication allows the corporation to set up against third parties, eventual ultra vires acts executed by directors when these acts are manifestly foreign to the objects clause.[50]

Indeed, delimiting the object allows confining the sphere of powers of corporate organs both the directors who can only perform those acts contemplated in the objects

---

is founded; however in a technical sense, anything related to it is understood as the object of the corporate contract, therefore, that is its *content*. In turn, such *content* is formed by the contributions of the associates, the executed commercial activity to obtain profits, and the distribution of these and the losses. Cf. Ferrara (1949), p. 147.

[47] Genghini (2012), pp. 9–10.

[48] Vivante (1932) §34. It is not strange that founding partners jot down as the objects clause any economic activity, but secretly executing other or neither. In the first scenario, the ultra vires doctrine could have room. In the latter, there is a simulated company (*società simulata*) or a company with a simulated objects clause. This is a trick to elude the creditors' rights transferring personal assets to the company or to avoid paying taxes. Cf. Cian (2017), p. 28.

[49] A comprehensive analysis about the legal concept of *commercial activity* in business law, in Ascarelli (1964), pp. 140–169.

[50] De Gregorio (1945), pp. 172–173, Brunetti (1960), p. 241.

clause (art. 2384, num. 1), and the powers of the general meeting whose decisions are valid whether adopted following the law and the articles of association (art. 2377, num. 1) and therefore respecting the objects clause. The general meeting cannot decide about a specific operation foreign to the objects clause, however, it might alter or even substitute the objects clause, nevertheless in doing so it establishes a new rule for upcoming cases.[51] It is not viable even one exception to the objects clause concerning a specific issue—such as the authorization and later ratification of a foreign act to the objects executed by directors—because such a decision shall be voidability accordingly to C.C. art. 2377.[52]

In relation with the joint-stock company, the *Codice Civile* provides that a significant amendment in the objects clause shall be valid only through an extraordinary general meeting, to safeguard the stockholders' interests who have agreed to the constitution of the firm. This is because it was aimed to execute a specific economic activity, and maybe those associates shall not be in accordance with another corporate purpose, therefore they have the right to demand respect for the original objects clause.[53]

According to C.C. art. 2328, num. 3, the SPA may be established by way of either a contract or a unilateral deed. The two chief features are: (i) a limited liability, and (ii) the corporate capital distributed in shares. The first principle has to deal with third parties, and the second, with the company relationship itself. The articles of association shall be drafted by public deed and shall specify the company's business purpose. The same provision applies to SRL.[54] Both provisions were recently modified by the Decree 6/2003. This was a relevant amendment because it clarified and specified the corporate's purpose in connection with the objects clause.

On the other hand, C.C. art. 2298 related to corporate representation provides:

> The administrator who represents the company can carry out all the acts that fall within the corporate purpose, subject to limitations resulting from the articles of association or the power of attorney. The limitations are not enforceable against third parties if they are not registered in The Company Register Office or if it is not proven that third parties have had any knowledge.

However, art. 2266, ibid. lays out in a general fashion that the company acquires the rights and assumes the obligations through the associates who have their representation. In the absence of a different provision in the corporate contract, the representation is due to each managing shareholder and extends to all relevant deeds

---

[51] See Paolini (2014), Chap. 1, for modern research about de facto alteration of the objects clause. In that monograph, a comparative study of this subject matter in Germany, the USA, and Holland also appears.

[52] Galgano (1999), pp. 244–245.

[53] Messineo (1971), p. 377. Italian company law is rooted in the conception of the corporation as a collective exercise of economic activity, based on the associates' will to perform a specific corporate purpose. Vid. Ferri (2000), pp. 249–250.

[54] C.C. art. 2463, num. 3. According to some scholars, all those acts performed beyond the corporate powers provided in the objects clause could be ratified by the general meeting. However, Italian courts considered those acts as wholly void, even if the general meeting wanted to ratify them unanimously. See, Martorano (1961), p. 7.

in the corporate purpose. The modifications and the extinction of the powers of representation are regulated in art. 1396, ibid.

According to Zanelli, when it comes to getting into the ultra vires doctrine, the interpreter must attend a double approach: firstly, to recognize that the subject matter is all about a statutory element related to the objects clause, and, in the second place, to look for the solution to this anomalous situation through another legal institution such as the company capacity or the representation powers of the administrative organ.[55] In that respect, Zanelli states that it is viable to preserve the validity of an ultra vires act applying the "theory of appearance" when the circumstances allow to configure an apparent legitimation upon a legitimating anomalous situation.[56]

4.5 Spain

According to the Spanish C.C. art. 35: "The following shall be legal entities: 1. Corporations (...). Their personality shall begin from the very moment in which they should have been validly incorporated in accordance with the law. (...)". In turn, art. 37, ibid., provides: "The civil capacity of corporations shall be governed by the laws which have created or recognized them. (...)". Finally, the first paragraph of art. 38, ibid. lays out: "Legal entities may acquire and possess property of all kinds, and contract obligations and exercise civil and criminal actions, in accordance with the laws and internal regulations".

Due to the lack of a clear precedent concerning the capacity of juristic persons, in particular, those in respect to commercial associations, likewise French legal corporate regime, in Spain a special capacity system prevails, taking into account the C.C. art. 36. In this way, being that the company capacity is regulated through their by-laws, the objects clause would confine such capacity. On the other hand, taking as starting point art. 38 ibid. it is possible to state that corporations have a general capacity not limited by the objects clause.[57]

In the last seventy years, Spain has had four corporate law regulations: Law of July 17, 1951; Law 19/1989; Decree 1564/1989; and, Decree 1/2010. The ancient law of 1951 laid out in art. 11, num. 3, that the articles of incorporation must contain the objects clause, and the objects clause confines the directors' representative powers. Therefore, the objects clause should be designed to fit the company's needs, in that respect they must be broad enough to encompass the commercial and industrial activities proposed. In turn, art. 77, allowed directors to perform any kind of act in connection with the objects clause, however, all individuals interested in a contractual relationship with the firm must be advised to ascertain that this specific act is listed in

---

[55] Zanelli (1962), pp. 375–376.

[56] Zanelli (1962), pp. 393. A modern and exhaustive approach about the theory of juristic appearance by Contreras (2006), pp. 482–486. In particular, the subject matter related to the apparent representation derived from the contract of mandate.

[57] Cf. Sáenz (1990), pp. 171–177, discussing this thesis.

the articles of incorporation. Thus, either if the act goes beyond the director's powers or is not listed in the articles of incorporation, it is considered as ultra vires.[58]

Before the enacting of Decree 1564/1989, it was argued by De La Cámara that by no means the ultra vires doctrine—as considered in common law systems—could have room in Spanish corporate law, because conversely to UK and USA, in Spain there was no mistrust towards juristic persons, even more, in the frame of a liberal ideology that inspired their Civil Code and Commercial Code, it was proclaimed that corporations were "new organisms created through the spontaneous forces of a society that progresses".[59] In that respect, the creditors' protection—as conceived by the ultra vires doctrine—does not have an equivalent in Iberian law. No one special measure is adopted when the objects clause changes, therefore there is not a relevant interest in the creditors' rights.[60]

According to Decree 1/2010, art. 23(b) related to stock corporations, the articles of incorporation must contain the objects clause determining its activities. This new law lays out that limited liability corporations will have an objects clause, pointing out:

> Art. 436(1). The new corporation shall have as its object clause all or some of the following activities, which will be transcribed literally in the articles of incorporation: agricultural, livestock, forestry, fishing, industry, construction, commerce, tourism, transportation, communications, intermediation, professional services or services in general.

As we can notice, Spanish legislators considered it appropriate to include a *numerus clausus* system in connection with commercial activities that such corporations could perform. However, the second paragraph provides:

> In addition, the founding members may include in the objects clause any singular activity other than the above. If the inclusion of such singular activity gives rise to a negative qualification by the mercantile registrar of the company deed of incorporation, its registration will not be paralyzed, which will be practiced without the singular activity in question, provided that the founding partners expressly consent to it in the deed of incorporation itself or later.

This paragraph allows corporate founding members to delimit in the objects clause a singular business activity that could be linked with those mentioned in the first paragraph. For example, whether a company would like to get involved in the transportation business as its chief activity, and later to specify what kind of transportation (e.g., goods or people) and if the service will be provided through maritime or airways. A long time ago it was noted a set of hardships to clarify even when the objects clause is properly determined. This issue arises from the perspective of the corporation founders about the future commercial activities, taking into account that, ab initio, there is some resistance to delimit into a narrow spectrum the object clauses

58 Garrigues (1953), pp. 222–224, De Solá (1957), pp. 352–356, Gay (1962), p. 361, Esturillo (1996), pp. 132–137.

59 De La Cámara (1977), 331.

60 Professor Girón (1976), p. 208, holds that it is not correct to maintain that German system has been introduced to Iberian corporate law because in this legal system provisions are referred to *powers* not to *capacity*. Therefore, the act provided in the objects clause but subject to a limitation binds to the corporation. However, nothing is directly said about a strange act to the objects clause.

because of the fear of falling into the ultra vires doctrine's turbulent waters. However, sometimes there has been agreement by corporators to leave an open-door policy to make a shift in the corporate activities, without the need to modify the articles of incorporation through expensive and dilated procedures.[61]

In turn, the third and final paragraph provides:

> In no case may those activities for which a form of Joint-Stock Company is required or those whose exercise implies a unique and exclusive object be included in the corporate purpose.

Therefore, this legal provision contemplates two restrictions regarding objects clause. Firstly, it makes a restriction on all those acts whose performance is attributed to joint-stock companies such as banking; and, on the other hand, there is a limitation for a corporation with a unique purpose such as public utilities.

Decree 1/2010 provides in art. 234, num. 1—with respect to the scope of representation power: "The representation will extend to all acts included in the objects clause defined in the articles of incorporation". This norm corresponds to the first paragraph of art. 129 of Decree 1564/1989. In the opinion of Sánchez, this norm contradicts Directive 68/151/CEE because in the communitarian regulation the objects clause does not confine the directors' representative powers, by contrast, the corporation shall be binding upon it even if those acts are not within its objects clause. In turn, the attribution of representative powers to the directors in a unitary and indivisible mode is incompatible with an ulterior delimitation of the scope of representation.[62]

On the other hand, art. 234, num. 2, provides: "Any limitation of the representative powers of the administrators, even if it is registered in the Mercantile Registry, will be ineffective to third parties". In turn, according to Directive 68/151/CEE, art. 9, num. 2: "The limits on the powers of the organs of the company, arising under the statutes or from a decision of the competent organs, may never be relied on as against third parties, even if they have been disclosed". As we can notice, apparently there is a correspondence between both provisions, however, the issue deals with the nature of the representative power limits. In this context, it must be understood that the ineffectiveness in connection with limitations of representative powers, should be circumscribed to those acts framed in the objects clause.

Lastly, art. 234, second paragraph, states: "The company will be liable to third parties who have acted in good faith and without gross negligence, even when it is clear from the articles of incorporation registered in the Mercantile Registry that the act is not included in the objects clause". By this provision Spanish legislators desired to protect third party interests, therefore it must be accredited that this third party acted in good faith and without gross negligence.

---

[61] De La Cámara (1977), p. 321.

[62] Sánchez (1996), pp. 2436–2437.

References

Andenas M et al (2009) European comparative company law, Cambridge
Andersson J (2015) The making of company law in Scandinavia and Europe. In: Fleischer H (ed) German and Nordic perspectives on company law, Tilbingen
Ascarelli T (1951) Principios y Problemas de las Sociedades Anónimas, México
Ascarelli T (1964) Iniciación al Estudio del Derecho Mercantil, Barcelona
Berr (1961) L'exercice du Pouvoir dans les Sociétés Comerciales, Paris
Breccia U et al (1995) Derecho Civil, t. 1, vol 1, Bogotá
Brunetti A (1960) Derecho de las Sociedades, t. 1, Buenos Aires
Burdeau G (1980) Droit Constitutionnel, Paris
Cian M (2017) Diritto Commerciale, vol 3, Torino
Contreras R (2006) Teoría Integral de la Apariencia Jurídica, México
Cozian M (2009) Droit des Sociétés. Paris
De Gregorio A (1945) Corso di Diritto Commerciale, Roma
De La Cámara M (1977) Estudios de Derecho Mercantil, vol 1, Jaén
De Solá F (1957) Tratado de Sociedades por Acciones, t. 1, Buenos Aires
De Vries H et al (1964) Limited liability contract: the GmbH. Columbia L Rev 64:866
Demogue R (1922) The impossibility of effecting contractual incompetence and its consequences. Yale L J 31
Enriques L (2006) EC company law directives and regulations. UPenn J Int Econ L 27
Ercklentz E (1981) The GmbH law amendments of 1980. Int L 15:645
Esturillo A (1996) Estudio de la Sociedad de Responsabilidad Limitada, Madrid
Feine (1930) Sociedades de Responsabilidad Limitada, Madrid
Ferrara F (1949) Empresarios y Sociedades, Madrid
Ferri G (2000) Manuale di Diritto Commerciale, Torino
Ferro P (2001) Contratti Associativi, Milano
Fischer R (1934) Sociedades Anónimas, Madrid
Galgano F (1999) Derecho Comercial, t. 2, Bogotá
García M (2002) Sociedad Anónima Europea, Madrid
Garrigues J et al (1953) Comentario a la Ley de Sociedades Anónimas, t. 1, Madrid
Gavalda C (2009) Sociétés Commerciales, Paris
Gay R (1962) Tratado de Sociedades Anónimas, Barcelona
Genghini L (2012) Società di Persone, Torino
Gierke O (1957) Derecho Comercial, vol 1, Buenos Aires
Girón J (1976) Derecho de Sociedades, Madrid
Guinnane T (2018) German company law 1794–1897. In: Research handbook on the history of corporate and company law, Cheltenham
Hauriou A (1971) Derecho constitucional, Barcelona
Hémard J et al (1974) Sociétés commerciales, t. 2, Paris
Houpin C et al (1935) Traité des Sociétés Commerciales, t. 1, Paris
Kuntz T (2018) German corporate law in the 20th century. In: Research handbook on the history of corporate and company law, Cheltenham
La Villa G (1996) Introduzione al Diritto Europeo delle Societa, Torino
Lettmaier S (2006) Die Ultra Vires-Lehre im Englischen Kapitalgesellschaftsrecht im Vergleich mit der Deutschen Entwicklung, Erlangen
Lyon-Caen (1908) Traité de Droit Commercial, t. 2, Paris
Magnier V (2013) Droit des Sociétés, Paris
Malepeyre L (1833) Traité des Sociétés Commerciales, Paris
Martorano F (1961) Capacità delle Società e Oggetto Sociale nel Diritto Anglo-americano. Napoli
Merle P (2005) Sociétés Commerciales, Paris
Messineo F (1971) Derecho Civil y Comercial, t. 5, Buenos Aires
Michoud L (1932) Théorie de la Personnalité Morale, pt. 2, Paris

Muchlinski P (2013) Development of German corporate law until 1990. German L J 14(2)
Paolini A (2014) Modificazioni di Fatto dell Oggetto Sociale. Milano
Pardessus J (1841) Cours de Droit Commercial, t. 4, Paris
Pic P (1908) Sociétés Commerciales, t. 1, Paris
Pistor K et al (2002) Evolution of corporate law. U Pa J Int Econ L 23:791
Pothier R (1764) Traité du Contrat de Société, Paris
Prélot M (1978) Droit Constitutionnel, Paris
Ripert G (2009) Traité Elémentaire de Droit Commercial, t. 1, vol 2. Paris
Sáenz J (1990) El Objeto Social en la Sociedad Anónima, Madrid
Sánchez H (1996) Objeto Social y Poder de Representación en la Sociedad Anónima. In: Estudios Jurídicos en Homenaje a Aurelio Menéndez, vol 2, Madrid
Schlesinger R et al (1998) Comparative law, New York
Schlink C (1935) Die Ultra Vires Lehre im Englischen Privatrecht, Berlin
Schlüter W (1991) Derecho de Sociedades en Alemania. In: Revista de Derecho Comercial, año 24, No. 142 a 144, Buenos Aires
Schmidt K (1997) Derecho Comercial, Buenos Aires
Schneider H et al (1996) German stock corporation act, München
Schulz M et al (2012) The law of business organizations: A concise overview of German corporate Law, Heidelberg, pp 26–30
Schuster E (1907) Principles of German civil law, Oxford
Serick R (1958) Apariencia y Realidad en las Sociedades Mercantiles, Barcelona
Troplong R (1843) Contrat de Société, t. 1, Paris
Ulmer P (1998) Derecho Alemán de Sociedades de Responsabilidad Limitada, Madrid
Vagts D (1966) Reforming the 'modern' corporation: perspectives from the German law. Harvard L Rev 80
Vivante C (1932) Tratado de Derecho Mercantil, vol 2, Madrid
Wolff M (1938) On the nature of legal persons. L Q Rev 54:494
Zanelli E (1962) Nozione di Oggetto Sociale, Milano

Chapter 5
The Ultra Vires Doctrine in Latin America

Abstract In this chapter, we study the ultra vires doctrine in corporate law from a Latin American perspective. Historically European Law has had a remarkable influence on the foundation and development of corporate law in Latin America. It is so noteworthy that, for instance, a couple of modern Colombian textbooks have seriously studied European corporate law (Cf. Juan Galindo. *Derecho europeo de sociedades*, Bogotá, 2002; and, Francisco Reyes. *Derecho societario en Estados Unidos y la Unión Europea*, Bogotá, 2013), and even the legal texts allow evidencing this situation. In the case of the corporate purpose and the objects clause, there are many similarities between them when comparing legal provisions, some derogated, and some others still in effect (Régimen de las Sociedades Anónimas en los Países de la ALALC (1971), pp. 153–158. A succinct comparative introduction about the ultra vires doctrine in EU, UK, USA, and Latin America, in Villegas (1997), pp. 240–247). With this in mind, we are going to make a comparative approach concerning the ultra vires doctrine and its validity in Latin America, taking into account that a lot of said about it in Europe likewise applies to Latin America.

5.1 Argentina

Argentinean corporate law was firstly regulated by the Commercial Code of 1859 and currently by Law 19.550 of 1972. With its successive amendments, this is the statute applicable to the business associations in the form of corporations. According to C.Co. art. 291: "The deed of partnership or company should contain the following details: ... (4) Specific designation of the class of business to be carried out by the company or partnership...". Halperin states that the objects clause had to be determined and its interpretation extensive. Since then, the objects clause was considered as an important device to delimit company capacity and the powers[1] of directors.

[1] Halperin (1958), pp. 22–24. The determination of the objects clause was only mandatory to joint-stock and limited liability companies; however, Law 19.550 made it extensive for any type of company. It would seem expedient to establish this rule in a general way, to avoid unscrupulous businesspersons from creating new corporations to commit frauds.

M. A. Jiménez Sánchez, *The Ultra Vires Doctrine in Corporate Law*,
SpringerBriefs in Law, https://doi.org/10.1007/978-3-030-88838-1_5

It is been submitted by Cabanellas that the ultra vires doctrine is foreign to the Argentinean's legal system not only because of a historical caprice.[2] Whether to execute acts with a corporation implies being cognizant of the objects clause under the risk that such kinds of acts could not be attributed to the company, and therefore it would be impossible for those firms to operate regularly in business. However, this assertion does not mean to deny that company capacity could be confined, the issue is to determine, in the light of the corporate law goals, to what extent it should be; thus, the associates should freely decide the commercial activities to undertake.[3]

As we said, in ancient French corporate law the directors were mandataries of the firm, therefore, they were granted broad powers to manage both affairs and corporate property. However a disagreement has arisen because in the case of joint-stock companies directors are not mandataries of the corporation, they only have the powers expressly granted by the firm and directly related to executive functions. In consequence, those inherent obligations to this position have to deal with the enforcement of the board's decisions, and these in respect to day-to-day activities in connection with the corporate affairs.[4]

Under this context the ultra vires doctrine has room in Argentinean corporate law, taking into account that Law 19.550, art. 11, num. 3, provides that by-laws must contain the objects clause in a precise and determined way.[5] Moreover, they must be also possible and lawful.[6] Another thesis holds that the ultra vires doctrine in Argentinean corporate law emerges from art. 54, third paragraph, ibid. In accordance with such a norm, when the company only endeavors the obtaining of extra corporate goals and becomes just a vehicle to violate the law, public order, good faith or to elude third party rights, it will be directly attributed to the associates or to the directors that allow it to happen, and who will be liable for the damages jointly and unlimitingly.

Thus, Argentinean policy-makers have used the concept of ultra vires as a basis for their approach to dealing with corporate personality issues. Certainly, there is no direct mention of the ultra vires doctrine but the phrase 'an act beyond the corporate goals' can be interpreted as an act that is made against the objective of the corporate

---

2 Cabanellas (1993), p. 303.

3 See footnote 2.

4 Alegría (1963), p. 135. According to Sasot Betes (1980), the directors might open a banking account, lease a building, hire and fire employees, draft negotiable instruments, etc. Alegría argues that this is only when a special mandate is conferred. However, corporate management implies the exercise of the objects clause. In that respect, the corporation is represented by the board, and not by the directors as individually considered. See, Martorell (1988), pp. 301–302. In joint-stock companies, there is also the position of manager. This person may be appointed to everyday tasks and in a diverse spectrum of activities; thus, there may be a manager for each department (e.g., legal, sales, investor relations, etc.). Cf. Richard et al. (1980), pp. 300–301.

5 Despite art. 11, num. 3 not expressly states it, the objects clause must also be *unique*, or, at least, just contain ancillary activities to the main object. This conclusion is reached after a holistic analysis of Law 19.550. Vid. Farina (2011), p. 182.

6 Richard et al. (1980), pp. 44–46. Upon such a basis, there is a difference also between objects clause and commercial activities. The first corresponds to the categories of transactions that any corporation may perform and delimits the field of affairs. The latter are those business transactions, and in general terms, the corporate life in action. See, Garrone (2008), p. 225.

entity presented in the memorandum of association. Through the registration of the memorandum of association, the corporate entity comes into existence. In this document, one of the requirements is to state the objective of the company. This is one of the conditions that should be met in order for the law to recognize the existence of the corporate entity. If a company acts against this objective, it should be considered as having acted beyond what was authorized by law. In practice, companies may be allowed to act beyond their original objective, since changing this objective may involve a burdensome process. However, this omission of formalities goes with a tacit condition, 'as long as it is not against public order'. Therefore, an act beyond corporate goals in this context should be interpreted as the use of the company as a tool for achieving fraud. Under this point of view, it is important to emphasize that the existence of a statutory rule, in addition to the willingness of the Argentinean judiciary to apply this remedy, has not meant that the disregard of the legal entity is a frequent practice in this jurisdiction. The Argentinean judiciary emphasizes the exceptional enforcement of the rule contained in art. 54, based on the premise that the uncontrolled application of this remedy may affect legal certainty and undermine the benefits of the corporate personality. In the case of *Pardini v. Fredel SRL*, the Argentinean judiciary drew attention to the fact that a remedy such as it is not opposable to the juristic personality "must be applied when it is proved that there has been a fraudulent use of the corporate entity and there is no other remedy available".[7]

On the other hand, art. 58, ibid. related to management and representation of joint-stock companies lays out that directors bind the corporation in connection with all those acts that are not notoriously foreign to the objects clause.[8] In the opinion of Cabanellas, this provision rejects the ultra vires doctrine in connection with corporate liability, nevertheless, it does not abandon it.[9] In turn, Roitman claims that the strict application of the classic version of the ultra vires doctrine would imply that any act performed by the directors, foreign to the objects clause cannot be attributed to the company.[10] This rule is attenuated by art. 58, mainly to protect third party's interests. Thus, in addition to the acts expressly contemplated in the objects clause, broad kinds of acts related to the company's purpose may also be attributed to the corporation. To verify if the act is notoriously foreign, the analysis must be done taking into account not only the objective aspect of it but their subjective aspect too in relation to third party attributes being cognizant of the objects clause and the usual commercial activities. Because of that, whether such an act is foreign but not "notoriously" so and recognizing the third party knew of it, it cannot be attributed to

[7] Lezcano (2017), p. 266.

[8] The Argentine Supreme Court has submitted that the reason behind the legal notion of acts "notoriously foreign" to the objects clause is to protect third parties who might be cheated if the law would allow denying them any kind of hypothetical statutory restrictions on behalf of the company. In re CNac.A.Com. Sala E, 23-03-99. In subsequent adjudications, the Court ruled that *contrario sensu*, when financial activities are included in the objects clause, such acts or transactions are not notoriously foreign because they are part of the corporate purpose. In re CNac.A.Com. Sala C, 14-07-06.

[9] Cabanellas (1993), pp. 305–306.

[10] Roitman et al. (2009), pp. 274–275.

the company because bad faith behaviors cannot be protected. Therefore, the criterion of interpretation must be broad, protecting a third party acting in good faith.[11]

It must be noted that in accordance with art. 274, ibid. the directors are responsible jointly and severally towards the company, the associates, and third parties, because: (i) a bad performance of their duties, (ii) the breaking of the law, or the by-laws, and (iii) any damage caused intentionally, by gross negligence, or in excess of their powers.

Zaldívar points out that this provision lays out two different kinds of liabilities: contractual and tort.[12] This distinction is important because of the burden of proof. Whether in presence of contractual liability, there is a presumption of culpability for the directors, on the contrary—i.e., tort—there is no such kind of presumption. Thus a bad performance of the duties, the transgression of the law or the by-laws in connection with the corporate matters, originates a contractual liability towards the associates. Conversely, a generic transgression of the law, intentional damages, abuse of powers, gross negligence, and any kind of liability about third parties becomes a tort.[13]

According to Colombres, one of the draftsmen of Law 19.550, the ultra vires doctrine was welcomed via art. 58, and must be interpreted in the light of Anglo-Saxon wide conception, i.e., as a limit to the corporate capacity and the power of the directors.[14] In this way, if the law demands a precise and determinate objects clause, it is easy to evidence which acts go beyond this scope. Therefore, as conceived in Argentinean corporate law, the ultra vires doctrine has an inside effect on the powers conferred to directors, and outside advising third parties that corporate representatives cannot celebrate any kind of contract or perform every desired transaction, but only those expressly authorized and directly related to the corporate objects. In consequence, such acts or transactions notoriously foreign to the objects clause cannot be attributed to the company, but in a personal manner to the directors.[15]

Lastly, let us take a look at the Argentinean SAS. With the enactment of Law 27.349 of 2017, a brand new type of corporation was included. According to art. 36, num. 4, substituted by Law 27.444 of 2018, art. 34, the articles of incorporation shall include, as one of the legal requirements, the stipulation of its *object*, which could be broad and pluralistic. The activities that integrate the objects clause may or may not be related to it. Through this type of company, some difficulty avoidance is assumed that arose from the other type of firms, such as ultra vires matters derived from a narrow objects clause. However, from our point of view, those matters continue.

---

[11] See footnote 10.

[12] Zaldívar et al. (1976), p. 526.

[13] See footnote 12.

[14] Colombres (1972), pp. 112–113.

[15] Colombres (1972), pp. 112–113, Aramouni (1994), pp. 9–11, Villegas (1997), pp. 238–239. The Argentine Supreme Court holds that when the corporation grants a surety in favor of its director, such an act is notoriously foreign and overcomes the objects clause, except whether the company has a financial purpose. In re CNac.A.Com. Sala B, 20-05-99.

Indeed, conversely to Colombian SAS,[16] in the Argentinean SAS the ultra vires doctrine has plenty of validity. In that jurisdiction, the possibility to draft a broad and pluralistic objects clause has always existed. In fact, as we mentioned previously, it is typical to include a long list of commercial activities as a means to avoid falling into ultra vires operations. The novelty could be that it allows listing unconnected activities in the objects clause. However, when the directors execute any act that is not described in such a clause, they become ultra vires. To sum up: connected or unconnected, even in the case of Argentine SAS the directors are confined to the objects clause and any kind of act beyond these limits are ultra vires.

5.2 Brasil

The structure of Brazilian corporate law dates back to 1850 when the only two business associations authorized by the Commercial Code were partnerships and joint ventures.[17] Art. 302, num. 4, provided that the articles of association, whether notarial or private, must contain a specific designation of the *object*. In turn, art. 316, first paragraph, lays out: "In an ordinary partnership, the name of the firm signed by any one of the acting partners who by the articles of partnership is entitled to use it binds all the partners jointly and severally as regards third persons and third persons as regards the partnership, even although it is his private transaction or that of a third person; cases where the firm name has been used in transactions foreign to the business stated in the articles of partnership being the only one excepted". Despite such regulation scarcity, Brazilian codification played a key role in the formation of commercial law in the most enlightened part of South America.[18] Because of the evolution of trade and particularly the arrival of some USA corporations, in 1891 Decree 424 related to joint-stock companies was enacted. According to art. 2:

> The following may be the *objects* of a joint-stock company: every kind of trade or industry, agricultural undertakings, and any and every kind of service of a commercial or civil nature, so long as it is not contrary to the law, to morality or public decorum. (italics supplied)

Thus, joint-stock companies were permitted to undertake virtually any class of commercial activity. Under this context, an ultra vires act is almost inconceivable since the companies were legally authorized to execute all of the commercial and

---

[16] Also in UNCITRAL, OAS projects, USA, and UK company law, the objects clause could be referred to simply as "any lawful activity". On the contrary, Argentine SAS did not follow this way, and therefore we can assert that the ultra vires doctrine is still in effect taking into account the manner that art. 36, num. 4, it was composed.

[17] In 1850, Brazil enacted into law its Commercial Code. This code was unique because it was the first commercial code adopted by a Latin American country that was not a servile copy of a European code. Although it closely followed the Portuguese Commercial Code of 1833, not a single provision was a replica of the Portuguese one; in fact, many of them were entirely authentic to the Brazilian Code. Vid. Swartz (1975), pp. 347, 353.

[18] Octavio et al. (1911), pp. 4–5.

industrial activities which then were taking place. That provisions with respect to corporations no longer obeyed fundamental ideas dominant at the time. Therefore, it was necessary to restructure the system from the cardinal principle of the corporation as a contract; in that respect, the company objects consisted of any type of human activity confined to the sphere of commercial law.[19] However, it was not until 1976 with the enactment of Law 6404 regarding joint-stock corporations, that Brazilian corporate law had a modern statute.[20] Under art. 2:

> The corporate purpose of a corporation may be any profit-making undertaking not contrary to law, public order, or decency.
>
> (...)
>
> Paragraph 2. The by-laws of a corporation shall define its corporate purposes in a precise and complete manner.

This provision requires a two-sided analysis. Firstly, the corporate purpose was indefinitely broad and only subject to being a profitable business (*animus lucrandi*), in consequence, excluding any charitable or non-profitable activity. In turn, it is not enough to be a profit-making undertaking; this must be in accordance with the law, public order, or decency. Secondly, as stated in par. 2, the by-laws shall define such corporate purpose in a complete and precise manner. This second paragraph allows for the appearance of the ultra vires doctrine in joint-stock corporations because when limiting the object to specific operations, those not listed become ultra vires.

In turn, art. 144, ibid. lays out the representation of the company, as follows:

> In the absence of a provision in the by-laws or a resolution of the administrative council, each director shall represent the corporation and take such actions as are necessary for its normal operation.
>
> Sole Paragraph. Within the limits of their duties and powers, the directors may appoint corporate attorneys and shall specify in the instrument of appointment the scope of their authority, and the period of their appointment which, in the case of a power of attorney to appear in court, may be for an indefinite period.

The first paragraph of this provision contemplates a command to directors to take action to achieve the corporate purpose as expressed in the objects clause. In turn, the second paragraph prescribes a key duty of directors: to appoint the company's lawyers, that will represent the firm in court and will give legal advice to the corporation in their best interests.

Nowadays with the enactment of the new Brazilian Civil Code (Law 10.406 of 2002), the regime of civil and business associations was unified. Likewise, it was provided in art. 47, as a general principle, that those acts exercised by directors within the limits of its powers defined in the constitutive act are binding on the legal entity. *Contrario sensu*, those ultra vires acts shall not bind the corporation, nevertheless, in accordance with the sole paragraph of art. 47, certain acts committed in excess of

---

[19] Mendonça (1963), pp. 20–21. For analysis about the juristic personality in Brazilian corporate law, and the correlative company's capacity, at pp. 76–97.

[20] See Bulgarelli (1976, 1981) for a briefing related to the ultra vires doctrine in Brazilian joint-stock companies.

powers also bind the firm.[21] Because of this provision, Pontes considers that the ultra vires doctrine is not only legally enforceable but transversal to any kind of business association or civil entity except in the case of a joint-stock corporation. However, a distinction must be made between acts executed with *abuse* of power, and those executed with an *excess* of power, so only in the first hypothesis shall this be ultra vires.[22]

The most relevant provision related to ultra vires doctrine comes from C.C. art. 1.015: "In the silence of the contract, the directors can practice all the acts pertinent to the management of the company; not constituting a corporate object, the encumbrance or sale of real estate depends on what the majority of the partners decide". In turn, the sole paragraph ibid. lays out: "Excess by the directors can only be opposed by third parties if at least one of the following hypotheses occurs: (i) if the limitation of powers is registered or registered in the company register; (ii) proving that it was known by the third party; (iii) in the case of an operation evidently foreign to company business objectives".

This provision has been subject to strong criticism, inasmuch as it blends in the same text different hypotheses whose legal consequences are also different. Indeed, Vieira observes that first part deals with the powers of the directors to perform management tasks, i.e., those intended to develop the objects, and in the next line alludes to some other acts that being extraordinary require the approval of shareholders.[23] Nevertheless, the sole paragraph jointly refers to those acts executed by directors with an excess of powers, and the ones performed outside of the objects clause (ultra vires). According to this interpretation, in the first hypothesis, there is a want of *power* and in the second a lack of *capacity*.

On the contrary to modern trends, Vieira claims that Brazilian legislators opted to honor their antique legal tradition, validating the ultra vires doctrine but with limited scope as provided in the third paragraph of art. 1.015.[24] Therefore, these acts evidently foreign to the company business objects can be set up against third parties; however, it is admissible the ratification of such ultra vires acts. Nevertheless, is controversial with regards to the required quorum to do so. One thesis claims that unanimity is needed, and the other points out that required quorum to alter the articles of association is required.[25]

Lastly, in the Enunciado 219 of the III Jornada de Direito Civil do Conselho da Justiça Federal, the following principles were proclaimed: The ultra vires doctrine applies in Brazilian law, with the following caveats: (a) the ultra vires acts do not have an effect only concerning corporations; (b) the company may ratify ultra vires acts through its deliberative body; (c) the Civil Code eased the ultra vires doctrine rigor, admitting the implied powers of directors to conduct accessories or business related to the corporate purpose, which do not constitute operations evidently foreign

[21] Vid. Vieira (2007), footnote 26.

[22] Pontes de Miranda (2012), pp. 416–417.

[23] Vieira (2007), pp. 32–33.

[24] Vieira (2007), pp. 40–42.

[25] See footnote 24.

to company objects; (d) C.C. art. 1015 does not apply to joint-stock companies, because there is a special rule with respect to such kind of director liability. Indeed, in the case of the joint-stock company, C.C. art. 1.089, lays out that these types of companies are still regulated by special laws.[26] Conversely, Oliveira considers that limited liability companies are integrally regulated by Civil Code, therefore, the ultra vires doctrine has a full effect regarding such companies.[27]

5.3 Colombia

Contemporary Colombian corporate law has as a starting point the enactment of the Commercial Code back in 1971 (Decree 410, March 27, 1971, to become effective as of January 1, 1972). This statute is divided into five books and regulates corporations in the Second Book, which is divided into two parts. The first deals with the corporate contract by way of general principles applied to any kind of corporation, and the second contains specific provisions for each class of company with its respective special principles. In this way, the Colombian legislator wanted to integrate into the same legal text a cumulative group of general provisions to the contrary of other jurisdictions such as Germany. With regard to the juristic person, the draftsmen proclaimed as a general principle, that all corporations (except de facto company) will have a juristic personality with capacity strictly limited to pertain to the usual and ordinary business carried out by that corporation, i.e., the business related with the objects clause.[28] Thus, since the first draft of the current Commercial Code published in 1958, the committee already had in mind that corporations cannot perform any kind of business, but only those expressly contemplated in their by-laws. Therefore, any other class of affairs outside of this ambit of competence is considered as ultra vires.

A few scholars have dedicated special working papers to study the ultra vires doctrine in Colombian corporate law and its connection with the objects clause, taking into account the "principle of specialty". Despite the ultra vires doctrine being born in foreign jurisdictions, from a detailed analysis of the Colombian company law system, it is possible to note their validity. To the extent that company capacity is given by the objects clause as expressly laid out in C.Co. art. 99, and if it is true that corporators are free to choose those acts which will make up part of the objects clause, once it is done they are limited to complying with it and making it comply.[29]

[26] See Gonçalves (2017), pp. 257–259, for a brief analysis of this new general regulation of civil and commercial law. The director liability in joint-stock companies was regulated in Law 6404 of 1976, art. 158. According to such provision: "An officer shall not be personally liable for the commitments he undertakes on behalf of the corporation and by virtue of action taken in the ordinary course of business; he shall, however, be liable for any loss caused when he acts: (i) within the scope of his authority, with fault or fraud; (ii) contrary to the provisions of the law or of the by-laws. (…)".

[27] Oliveira (2012), 118.

[28] Ministerio de Justicia (1958), t. 2, pp. 87, 91.

[29] Bernal et al. (1991), pp. 68–69.

The most relevant technical aspect of the juristic personality is the separation of corporate property and the personal property of the associates. Historically, patrimony is considered a guaranty mechanism for creditors, in the case of a company this principle implies a reinforced application taking into account the sort of risks assumed in everyday business life. To the extent that corporate contract gives birth to the company, at the same time it fixes their limits to capacity as a juristic person. It is recognized that corporations have full capacity. However, this is circumscribed to these acts and transactions strictly determined in the objects clause. Consequently, the want of capacity is only predictable in the light of those businesses executed and not expressly listed in the objects clause or not directly related to them.[30]

To sum up, Colombian corporate law recognizes that once lawfully incorporated, the company constitutes a different juristic person out of the associates individually considered, and any act beyond the corporate capacity is void. Therefore, the corporate contract both originates the company and determines the limits to its capacity as a juristic person. These principles are reunited in the C.Co. art. 99:

> The capacity of the company will be limited to the development of the company or activity foreseen in its object. Acts directly related to it and those aimed at exercising rights or fulfilling obligations, legally or conventionally derived from the existence and activity of the company, shall be understood as included in the corporate purpose.

This provision contemplates three kinds of acts: (i) those listed as principals in the objects clause; (ii) those not enunciated but with a direct relationship; and, (iii) any act not directly related with the objects clause, but necessary to enforce the rights and fulfill the obligations. Welcoming the French theory of *spécialité*, the Colombian legislation laid out that conversely to natural persons, corporations would have a capacity limited to and by the objects clause. The usual and ordinary business carried out by the corporation deals with everyday activities executed by the corporation in connection with the three scenarios previously mentioned. In this way, any act or transaction outside this violates the theory of *spécialité* because of the lack of capacity and becomes ultra vires.[31]

Reyes notices that determining the sphere of company capacity is one of the most complex matters in corporate law. Therefore, it will be necessary to specify on a case-by-case basis if the act or transaction has a direct relationship with the objects clause.[32] At this point, it is worth mentioning money loans between the company and its corporators as an ultra vires transaction. As we stated, USA courts held that a donation made by a company to a non-commercial entity is not ultra

---

[30] Pinzón (1989), pp. 201–203.

[31] Narváez (2008), pp. 24–26. This author illustrates an ultra vires case when a corporation does not contemplate in its by-laws the possibility to associate with another company, and, nevertheless, does it. This act is an absolute nullity and can be challenged in court by either corporators or any third party. However, Narváez enlists five hypotheses in which a company could associate with other companies. Op. cit., p. 139.

[32] Reyes (2006), p. 148.

vires[33]; however, the judges are more reluctant when an associate borrows money from his own company. In this scenario, USA courts consider that there must be a direct relationship between the loan and the corporate purpose to avoid falling into an ultra vires act. This line of thought is seconded by Colombian courts and authors who assume as ultra vires those kinds of transactions, which likewise are not contemplated in the objects clause, and also do not have a direct nexus between the credit and the corporate purpose.[34]

Indeed, C.Co. art. 110, num. 4, lays out that the incorporation document must contain the by-laws of the company and include the corporate purpose. This clause must indicate the main activities that the company will carry out and binds the legal capacity of the company. Corporations cannot have an undetermined purpose except as a general principle the SAS. This provision alludes to the objects clause, and also rules that any stipulation making it indeterminate or without a direct relationship with the objects clause will be invalid. Narváez recognizes that the objects clause becomes the backbone of a corporation with juristic personality.[35] The objects can be unique or exclusive when only alluding to a specific branch of business, and multiple when involving a variety of affairs. Also, it could be ancillary to the main object.[36] The objects clause is not only relevant to determine the company's capacity but also to limit the powers of the directors.

It is unanimously admitted the validity of the ultra vires doctrine in Colombian corporate law, taking into account many provisions contained in the Commercial Code.[37] Indeed, according to art. 190, decisions adopted in excess of the corporate contract limits shall be wholly void. Thusly, if the objects clause limits the corporate capacity then ultra vires acts do not have validity. Therefore, whether the objects clause determines the corporate limits, the ultra vires acts cannot have validity. In turn, art. 196 lays out that the directors will represent the company, according to the stipulations contained in the by-laws, and it is assumed that they shall be able to enter into a contract or perform any kind of act contemplated in the objects clause. As is

---

[33] AP Smith Manufacturing Co. v. Barlow, 13 N.J. 145, 98 A. 2d 581 (N.J. 1953). The Colombian mercantile regime contemplates as a cardinal principle the *animus lucrandi* in every business transaction; however, according to C.Co. art. 446, num. 3, lit. (c) is admissible to donate money and goods to both natural and juristic persons.

[34] Reyes (2006), pp. 149–150. However, this author stresses that in the light of Colombian Law 222 of 1995, art. 22, even if there was a middle-to-end relationship between the loan and the main corporate object, the directors could still be liable whether damage is caused to the company resulting from such loan, taking into account the duties of caution and loyalty.

[35] Narváez (2008), pp. 136–137. According to this author, the diversification of business without a direct relationship to the main object, even if they are related or complementary, is not in accordance with the principle of *specialty*.

[36] C.Co. art. 196, the second paragraph provides: "In the absence of stipulations, it shall be understood that the persons who represent the company may celebrate or execute all the acts and contracts included within the corporate purpose or those directly related to the existence and operation of the company".

[37] Bernal (1980), pp. 65–66, Gaviria (1984), pp. 109–111, Pinzón (1989), pp. 201–203, Reyes (2006), pp. 250–254, Gil (2012), pp. 38–42, Narváez (2008), pp. 139–141, Martínez (2020), pp. 202–206.

evidenced, this is an application of the ultra vires doctrine concerning the directors' powers. In the same way, art. 438 provides that the board of directors can order entering into a contract or performing any kind of act contemplated in the objects clause. Finally, art. 306 points out that the corporation will only be bound for those operations contemplated in the objects clause, and authorized by the company name or signature of the individuals empowered by it.

It is expedient to mention the case in which, despite having broad-ranging faculties, the directors cannot exercise their power to execute some acts because by doing so, such acts become ultra vires. For instance, the director of a financial institution operating in Colombia cannot transfer the whole or a significant part of the corporation's assets, debts, and contracts without previous and express authorization regardless of the broad scope of the mandate conferred thereon. In this case, an extraordinary mandate is required and must be granted either by the general shareholder meeting or be provided by special legislation.[38]

If there is a consensus about the validity of the ultra vires doctrine in Colombian company law, however, there is not about its legal effects. It must be borne in mind that no legal statutory provision determines its consequences. Because of this, Gaviria suggests that when the director performs an act that is part of the object clauses but does it either in the absence of express power or beyond it, there is no nullity but it cannot go against the company.[39] In this case, the director commits his liability as long as the third party would act in good faith according to that set forth in C.Co. art. 841. Therefore, the company's lack of capacity and consequently nullity will only arise when the corporations make a contract outside of the objects clause, or not directly related to it.[40]

In turn, another line of thought addressed by Bernal indicates that because this is an issue in respect to the capacity, the legal sanction must be nullity; however, a distinction must be made: (a) there will be absolute nullity when the act goes beyond the company's capacity in the framework of the objects clause because the ratification is not allowed and the protection in this scenario targets third parties, more than the company or its associates; and, (b) when the limits of the company organs are exceeded the ratification will always be allowed to the extent that they are

---

[38] This hypothesis applies to general partnership (C.Co. art. 316) and the SAS (Law 1258 of 2008, art. 32). It is expedient to notice that a corporation, however, having been created, is not dissolved, in contemplation of law, without a legislative or judicial act—or act in pursuance of legislative authority—extinguishing its franchises. So long as they exist, the corporation exists. Consequently, while the sale of the entire property of a corporation may render it unable to fulfill the purposes of its organization, it does not dissolve it. "A corporation may exist without property". See, Noyes, 226. In this regard, the courts have stated: "The sale of all the property may have the effect of terminating the business for which the corporation was organized, but it does not dissolve it. Such a sale no more dissolves the corporation than would the giving of a mortgage that might ultimately result in all the property being taken from the corporation". In re, Price v. Holcomb, 89 Iowa, 137 (1893), (56 N. W. Rep. 407).

[39] Gaviria (1984), p. 111.

[40] See footnote 39.

beneficial to the corporation. In this case, the protection is about both the firm and the corporators taking into account that this is an inside issue of the company.[41]

On the other hand, when the act is performed outside the objects clause, i.e., when the corporation's limits are exceeded, it becomes a matter of a lack of capacity; in consequence, the act must be void. Therefore, when the corporate capacity scope goes beyond the objects clause, there is absolute nullity, taking into account that such an act cannot be ratified and because the protection is focused on third party interests more than the corporation itself or the shareholders.[42] Conversely, when the directors or the board go beyond their powers, it is possible to ratify such an act on the condition that it benefits the corporation. In this case, it is all about the inside business of the firm. However, when third parties are harmed, they could file a suit for damages against the company.

Taking into account that corporate capacity is limited through the objects clause, the acts executed beyond such capacity make the firm non-liable, except when some associate commits its patrimony for an ample scope. This is, for instance, the case contemplated in the C.Co. art. 353, num. 2, which provides that in the limited liability company (Ltda.) the articles of incorporation may stipulate for all or some of the associates a greater responsibility. To sum up, all of the acts not stipulated in the articles of association and consequently outer of the corporation's capacity cannot bind the firm, even if they are performed by its directors. *Contrario sensu*, when the act is contemplated in the articles of association but the directors make an excess in its performance, it could be ratified.

Finally a special mention to Law 1258 of 2008, concerning the simplified joint-stock company (SAS). According to Professor Reyes, the starting point for the original proposal of SAS was the idea of facilitating the formalization of business entities and updating the legal system to introduce forward-looking approaches to corporate law.[43]

This brand new type of company is an important tool for economic growth, to the point that on June 20, 2017, the General Assembly of the OAS adopted a resolution regarding the Model Law on the SAS approved by the CJI. Mindful of the contribution

[41] Bernal (1980), pp. 65–66.

[42] Colombian Supreme Court of Justice has ruled in a judgment of July 27, 1978, that an ultra vires act is wholly void because of the lack of capacity. Subsequently, in a judgment of April 27, 1989, the theory of nullity was upheld but in this case not in connection with the lack of capacity but rather because of an unlawful object even when the firm's objects clause was lawful. However, in the opinion of Pinzón (1989), pp. 252–253, that nullity arising from an ultra vires act is avoidable, and, in consequence, could be ratified, reforming the by-laws to include such an act or transaction in the objects clause, in this way, it will be no more ultra vires, but a business into the scope of company's capacity. Op. cit., 203. On the contrary, other scholars consider that such ultra vires acts or transactions are wholly void because of the C.Co. art. 899, which lays out that when an act or contract goes against a mandatory rule, it shall be wholly void, except when the law provides another thing. See, Bernal, Desviaciones, op. cit., p. 70. In turn, Professor Reyes does not take sides but looks critically at the convenience of the ultra vires doctrine because it could become a source of juristic instability to the extent that the company's acts and contracts will be exposed uncertainly, and could be challenged in court at any time.

[43] Reyes (2015), p. 396.

that these new forms of companies may make to economic development, the General Assembly resolved to take note of the Model Law and requested the CJI and the Department of International Law to disseminate the Model Law as widely as possible. The Model Law provides a simplified corporate structure, extending the benefits of incorporation to many small and medium-sized business enterprises without the complexity and cost that is frequently required under existing domestic legislation in the Americas. This simplified model can also benefit larger businesses that seek expansion into international markets and facilitate foreign investment. The Model Law was inspired by the successes of Law 1258 of 2008 that introduced the SAS to Colombian company law.[44]

Indeed, as something innovative, Law 1258 of 2008 does not require the parties to provide for a restricted purpose clause in the by-laws. Thus, as a default rule, the law allows the corporation to be set up for any lawful purpose. According to research conducted by the Chamber of Commerce in 2011, most of the SAS set up in the capital city (i.e., Bogotá) prefer the flexibility afforded by the unlimited purpose clause to the rigidities of self-imposed restricted objects. A smaller percentage of SAS opted for limited purpose clauses by specifying restricted business activities in the corporation's by-laws. Interestingly, during the period between January 2009 and July 2013, a total of 2.162 amended their internal rules to insert in their objects the phrase "any lawful activity." This represents a preference for flexibility and demonstrates that the traditional system was inconsistent with entrepreneurs' needs and preferences.[45] Under this context, it is correct to affirm that in the Colombian SAS the ultra vires doctrine does not have validity because according to Law 1258, art. 5, num. 5, the contract or unilateral act of constitution must indicate: "A clear and complete statement of the main activities *unless it is stated that the company may carry out any lawful commercial or civil activity*. If nothing is expressed in the act of constitution, it will be understood that the company may carry out *any lawful activity*" (italics added). However, the ultra vires doctrine applies when the corporations delimit their objects clause and perform any act beyond them.[46]

---

[44] http://www.oas.org/en/sla/dil/newsletter_Model_Law_Simplified_Corporation_Report_Jul-2017.html [last accessed: 12/Sept/2021].

[45] Reyes (2015), pp. 415–416. Although according to the regulation governing the SAS there is no need to define any specific business purpose in the corporation's purpose clause, the Mercantile Registry keeps a record of these entities' main economic activity. The statistical data shows that the SAS model is mostly used for agricultural economic activities, manufacturing undertakings, construction business, and commercial activities (wholesale and retail). Ibid., p. 407.

[46] This "*any lawful activity*" purpose clause, as a statutory provision, was enacted in the MBCA and today every American jurisdiction permits the incorporation under general laws for any lawful purpose, except for certain regulated businesses. For a detailed background of this legislation, vid. Schaeftler (1983), footnote 33. In Spanish corporate law having the ancient regime of 1989 in force—and even before it—scholars were unanimously doubtless about the unlawfulness of this kind of undetermined clause. Vid. Rodríguez (1991), p. 163.

To avoid such illegality and with the purpose of having a *generic* objects clause, some corporations adopted one of the following mechanisms: (i) a prolix description encompassing all of the economic activities to be performed by the firm including commercial, industrial, and financial

5.4 México

Because of the geographic proximity to the USA, it was to be assumed that Mexican company law should be more related to common law than civil law. Nevertheless, from the Colonial period until the present time, Spanish legislature—such as the Commercial Code of 1829—has had a notorious influence, and it was not until 1854 when the first Mexican Commercial Code was promulgated. In art. 235 for the very first time in this country the ultra vires doctrine was contemplated, taking into account that all of the obligations bound by an associate-director, might be set up against the company even if such director had acted in contradiction to corporate instructions.[47]

Barrera points out that as a matter of principle, Mexican corporations are provided with a general capacity not confined by either its purpose or object but only limited to legal restrictions or those listed in the by-laws. In consequence—except where the charter has been amended—the company cannot violate such restrictions performing unauthorized acts. This shall be the only hypothesis to arise regarding the ultra vires doctrine in Mexican corporate law.[48] Indeed, corporations have plenty of capacity to get involved in any kind of business; nevertheless, as Rodríguez notices such capacity is not unlimited because in accordance with the C.C. art. 26 and General Law of Corporations of 1934, art. 10, the exercise of capacity must be in consonance to the ends proposed at the time of constitution.[49]

Upon this context, the ultra vires doctrine has plenty of validity taking into account that according to the Mexican General Law of Corporations of 1934, art. 6, num. 2, the by-laws must contain the objects clause, and these should be clear, concise, and ample. In turn, art. 10, ibid. lays out that representation of any company shall be the responsibility of its directors, who may perform all kinds of operations inherent to the objects clause, except as expressly provided by the law or corporate contract.[50]

---

business; or, (ii) a narrower but more profiled listing of economic activities, with subsequent addition of ancillary to the main objects clause activities. This second method is not correct because it creates confusion between economic activities, and legal devices to achieve them. Vid. De La Cámara (1977), p. 321. An analysis and detailed listing of the five most common undetermined objects clause, in Broseta (1971), footnote 23.

In the field of law of agency, before European Communities Act 1972—which protects third parties in certain cases—it was considered that a corporation cannot appoint an agent for any purpose, or to do any act, which is ultra vires in its memorandum of association. The contract entered into by the agent on the corporation's behalf, would not bind the corporation, and if the purpose of the appointment was specific, any contract with the agent would not be so either. But a corporation may perhaps be liable for an ultra vires tort committed by an agent. Cf. Bowstead (1985), p. 32. A description of lifting the corporate veil in English case law related to agency and the abuse of corporate personality that could trigger ultra vires acts, in Verrucoli (1964), pp. 103–114.

[47] Barrera (1984), 186. Later it was enacted the current Commercial Code of 1890.

[48] Barrera (1966), p. 41.

[49] Rodríguez (1978), p. 116.

[50] When enforcing the Mexican Commercial Code of 1889 related to corporations, i.e., before 1934, the articles having been properly registered in the place wherein the company is doing business, the acts committed in the name of the company, but in excess of its object (ultra vires), will not be binding upon the company, as notice of such objects is imparted through registration. But a failure

In this way, when the corporate purpose is diverted because of abusive use of powers due to the excess of those attributed (incompetence), or because such powers are granted to any other corporate organ (lack of legitimation), a civil action could arise looking for indemnity derivate of damages suffered.[51]

It is submitted that corporate representation is necessary and continuous. It is necessary since it ought to have human beings acting on behalf of it and continuously because even if they have legal capacity, it is through their 'organs' that they could exercise the rights and acquire obligations. It is contended that corporations have a general capacity not limited to their purpose; therefore, only legal restrictions and those stipulated in the corporate contract could impose a barrier in the firm's business activity. In that respect, to perform an act against such prohibitions will be ultra vires. According to C.C. art. 2716, however, the obligations acquired by directors-partners on behalf of the corporation, exceeding their powers, if not ratified, shall only bind the corporation for the benefits received. Thus, even if the act exceeds the objects clause, the general meeting could authorize the firms' legal representative to perform it. Of course, this ratification does not apply to illegal activities.[52]

The directors' powers must be in connection with the accomplishment of duties, and particularly having in mind the correct running of the business, as the primary aim. Consequently, inasmuch as those directors are empowered by the corporate bodies, they could achieve those goals. Taking into account such an end, MGLC, art. 10, proclaims that the company's representation will be in charge of directors who may execute any kind of operations inherent to the objects clause, and only under limitations imposed in the law or by-laws.

This provision has an immediate antecedent in Italian law, however, in Italy, the approach differs because it contemplates a negative proposition: directors cannot perform more operations than those listed in the articles of association. Conversely, Mexican corporate law provides the opposite: directors can and have to execute any class of operations to achieve the company's purpose not only management tasks. Nevertheless, these powers have intrinsic limitations such as the prohibition to sell the only company factory, because this would be an ultra vires act since this property allows for achieving the corporate purpose.[53] Anyway, when the directors act beyond

---

to effect such registration will make the company liable, even if its object has been exceeded. On the other hand, when an officer of the company has, in its name, effected a binding operation beyond such an object, and without the consent of the stockholders, he will be responsible to the company for any losses resulting therefrom. Vid. Fuller (1911), p. 24.

[51] Galindo (1986), pp. 980–981. On the other hand, Rodríguez (1978), pp. 127, 137–138, considers that an ultra vires transaction is not an excess of power but negligent contracting. Thus, those ultra vires acts could be challenged by the corporation through the individuals designed by the general meeting as the empowered corporate organ to do so against the current or former directors.

[52] Barrera (1967), pp. 156–158. According to this author, the corporation has no liability because the acts—lawful or unlawful—have been performed in excess by their director and beyond the objects clause or against the articles of incorporations or legal provisions that prohibit or limit such acts, except when the corporation has authorized, tolerated or ratified them. Conversely, the corporation becomes a liability by the acts of the directors—lawful or unlawful—performed in the frame of the objects clause. Op. cit., p. 186.

[53] Rodríguez (1978), t. 2, pp. 103–104.

the company capacity, the ultra vires doctrine comes into effect; however, there is no consensus about the nature of such irregularity. Thus, three probable solutions are contemplated:

(i) The absolute nullity of those acts, taking into account both the lack of capacity and the principle of specialty. Under this theory, MGLC, art. 10, contemplates two hypotheses: those acts performed by directors not framed in the objects clause (ultra vires) and those acts against that which is expressly provided in the law or stipulated in the corporate contract. This second class of acts in a narrow sense cannot be considered as ultra vires, but just as a violation of contractual inside limits imposed on the directors.[54]

(ii) Another thesis holds that such acts must be treated as if the company was 'irregular'. An 'irregular' company is one not registered but publicly acting regardless of not having fulfilled the legal requirements for its constitution. In that respect, those acts executed by a company not directly connected to the achievement of the corporate purpose might be comparable to those performed by an irregular company.[55]

(iii) The third theory considers that there is no nullity, but such ultra vires operations cannot be set up against the company; however, they could be ratified either expressly or tacitly by the competent organ (e.g., the general meeting, stockholders, etc.). Thus, the corporation could file a suit against the directors that acted beyond their powers, or in absence of them, to obtain monetary compensation for damages suffered.[56] On the other hand, it is submitted by Cervantes, that if an ultra vires act is not affected by a specific cause of nullity, such an act is unlawful but not nullity. In consequence, the sole circumstance of not being listed in the objects clause cannot be enough to predicate its nullity.[57]

5.5 Perú

Professor Laroza holds that ultra vires doctrine is not applicable in Perú, upon the basis that legal effects about acts not related to the objects clause are different from those analyzed and ruled in common law courts. Another argument deals with the fact that shareholders are the only ones competent to decide if the board or the directors have executed acts beyond their powers and if because of it, the firm has suffered patrimonial damage. Likewise in Perú, there is not an exhaustive objects clause, but

[54] Frisch (1994), p. 100. In fact, according to this author, such kinds of ultra vires acts cannot be ratified through a retroactive statutory alteration of the by-laws.

[55] Mantilla (1989), p. 210. However, this writer in a previous book related to negotiable instruments stressed that on behalf of a company, this cannot warrant the payment of a promissory note or bill of exchange, if such an act is not listed in the objects clause because it becomes ultra vires. See, Mantilla (1977), p. 180.

[56] Barrera (1983), pp. 86–87.

[57] Cervantes (1980), p. 45.

an enunciative one, that allows for including every kind of business or transaction.[58] Thus, according to Peruvian General Law of Corporations (Law 26.887 of 1997) art. 11:

> The corporation limits its activities to those lawful businesses or operations whose detailed description constitutes its objects clause. Acts related to it that contribute to the realization of its purposes are understood to be included in the objects clause, even if they are not expressly indicated in the articles of incorporation. The corporation cannot have the purpose of developing activities that the law attributes exclusively to other entities or people.

Taking into account such a provision, we can conclude that ultra vires doctrine has plenty of validity, but the legislator presumes that any ancillary act to the main object is included in the objects clause. This is nothing more than the ancient rule of connection between the main object and those which are ancillary.

References

Alegría H (1963) Sociedades Anónimas, Buenos Aires

Aramouni A (1994) El Objeto en las Sociedades Comerciales, Buenos Aires

Barrera J (1966) La Representación, No. 7

Barrera J (1967) Representación Voluntaria en Derecho Privado, México

Barrera J (1983) Temas de Derecho Mercantil, México

Barrera J (1984) Historia del Derecho de Sociedades en México. In: Estudios Jurídicos en Memoria de Roberto Mantilla, México

Bernal R (1980) Sociedad Anónima, Bogotá

Bernal R et al (1991) Desviaciones del Objeto Social en la Empresa Colombiana. Revista de Derecho Comercial, año 24, No. 142 a 144, Buenos Aires

Bowstead (1985) Law of agency, London

Broseta M (1971) Cambio de Objeto y Ampliación de Operaciones. In: Estudios Jurídicos en Homenaje a Joaquín Garrigues, vol 1, Madrid

Bulgarelli W (1976) Implicações da Teoria Ultra Vires Societatis na Lei 6.404/76

Bulgarelli W (1981) A Teoria Ultra Vires Societatis Perante a Lei das Sociedades por Ações. Revista Forense, ano 77, v. 273

Cabanellas G (1993) Derecho Societario, t. 2, Buenos Aires

Cervantes R (1980) Derecho Mercantil, México

Colombres G (1972) Curso de Derecho Societario, Buenos Aires

De La Cámara M (1977) Estudios de Derecho Mercantil, Jaén

Diez A (1996) Función e Importancia del Objeto Social en las Sociedades Mercantiles, Ius et Veritas No. 13, Lima

Farina J (2011) Sociedades Comerciales, t. 1, Buenos Aires

Frisch W (1994) Sociedad Anónima, México

Fuller D (1911) Law of Mexican commercial corporations, México

Galindo I (1986) El Órgano de Administración de la Sociedad Anónima, Cuadernos del Instituto de Investigaciones Jurídicas UNAM, Año 1, No. 3, México

Garrone J (2008) Derecho comercial, t. 1, Buenos Aires

---

58 Laroza (1995), p. 87. Peruvian scholars, however, recognize that ultra vires doctrine has a notable influence in common law and civil law systems, even if its validity causes controversy. Therefore, the law's evolution allows claiming that all those acts executed in excess of powers may be ratified for all of the shareholders. Vid. Diez (1996), 169.

Gaviria E (1984) Sociedades en el Código de Comercio, Bogotá
Gil J (2012) Derecho Societario Contemporáneo, Bogotá
Gonçalves C (2017) Direito Civil Brasileiro, t. 1, São Paulo
Halperin I (1958) Manual de Sociedades Anónimas, Buenos Aires
Laroza E (1995) Actos Ultra Vires en Sociedades Anónimas, Themis No. 87, Lima
Lezcano J (2017) Piercing the corporate veil in Latin America. In: Tomasic R (ed) Routledge handbook of corporate law, London
Mantilla R (1977) Títulos de Crédito Cambiarios, México
Mantilla R (1989) Derecho Mercantil, México
Martínez N (2020) Cátedra de Sociedades, Bogotá
Martorell E (1988) Sociedades Anónimas, Buenos Aires
Mendonça J (1963) Direito Comercial Brasileiro, vol 3, bk. 2, pt. 3, Rio de Janeiro
Ministerio de Justicia (1958) Proyecto de Código de Comercio, t. 2, Bogotá
Narváez J (2008) Teoría General de las Sociedades, Bogotá
Octavio R et al (1911) Commercial laws of the World, vol 4, London
Oliveira V (2012) Inovações do Novo Código Civil Referentes às Sociedades Limitadas. In: Segundo Congresso Brasileiro de Direito Comercial, São Paulo
Pinzón G (1989) Sociedades Comerciales, t. 1, Bogotá
Pontes de Miranda (2012) Direito Privado, t. 1, São Paulo
Régimen de las Sociedades Anónimas en los Países de la ALALC (1971) Buenos Aires
Reyes F (2006) Derecho Societario, t. 1, Bogotá
Reyes F (2015) Colombian simplified corporation. Penn State J Law Int Aff 4:392
Richard E et al (1980) Manual de Derecho Societario, Buenos Aires
Rodríguez J (1978) Tratado de Sociedades Mercantiles, t. 1, México
Rodríguez F (1991) Determinación Estatutaria del Objeto Social. In: Alonso A (coord) Derecho de Sociedades Anónimas, t. 1, Madrid
Roitman H et al (2009) Manual de Sociedades Comerciales, Buenos Aires
Sasot Betes M (1980) Sociedades Anónimas. El Órgano de Administración, Buenos Aires
Schaeftler M (1983) Ultra vires – ultra useless. J Corp Law 9:81
Swartz WR (1975) Brazilian commercial code of 1850. Tex Int Law J 10:347
Verrucoli P (1964) Superamento della Personalità Giuridica delle Società di Capitali nella Common Law e nella Civil Law, Milano
Vieira M et al (2007) Vinculação da Sociedade, Revista de Direito Mercantil, No. 146
Villegas C (1997) Sociedades Comerciales, t. 1, Buenos Aires
Zaldívar E et al (1976) Cuadernos de Derecho Societario, t. 2, pt. 2, Buenos Aires

Chapter 6
The Objects Clause and the Ultra Vires Doctrine

Abstract This chapter presents the fundamental concept of the objects clause and its close relationship with the ultra vires doctrine in corporate law. As we learned previously, alongside the company's capacity, the objects clause is the cornerstone of the ultra vires doctrine for all juristic systems researched in this writing. Therefore, in this section, we are going to study this subject matter in detail. Although the ultra vires doctrine was concerned with limiting the activities of a company within its stated *objects*, it necessarily had the effect also of restricting the company's *powers*. Nevertheless, as Sealy et al. (Cases and materials in company law, Oxford, p. 87, 2013), notes the line between objects and powers is a difficult—perhaps impossible—one to draw.

According to Maria the provisions that must be mentioned in the objects clause are of three kinds[1]: (i) the main provisions which are the heart of the company, and determinate the main object of the company as indicated in the name of the company. Around these provisions gravitate all the others. It is to this part of the object that most of the statutes are addressed when they are stipulated in the articles of incorporation relating to the extraordinary general meeting, that it cannot be altered in its essence; (ii) the ancillary and subsidiary provisions resulting from the main object of which they are the corollaries and consequences. For example, a company established for the manufacture of specified products has as accessory objects the purchase of raw material, and any other kind of commercial, industrial, and financial operations required by the operation of the company; (iii) any other provisions that provide for the participation of the company to other matters related to its object through the creation of new companies (e.g., mergers, etc.).

The objects clause defines the company's capacity and delimits what the company is legally capable of doing, whether it acts through its board, via the shareholders collectively, or through an agent. However, because of CA 2006, in the UK there is no longer a provision requiring a company to set up its objects. Unless it chooses otherwise, the company's objects will be unrestricted, it will have unlimited capacity.

[1] Maria (1906), 83.

M. A. Jiménez Sánchez, *The Ultra Vires Doctrine in Corporate Law*, SpringerBriefs in Law, https://doi.org/10.1007/978-3-030-88838-1_6

Even if a company chooses to adopt restrictions on its capacity, those restrictions will not affect the validity of the acts of the company, under s. 39(1).[2] Thus, Gower considers that the ultra vires doctrine, so far as it is based on the company's object clause, no longer threatens the security of third party transactions.[3]

However, as Smith explains if a company adopts an objects clause to limit its capacity, the ultra vires doctrine will remain relevant internally, i.e., with respect to deciding whether its directors have exceeded their powers and entered into a transaction that is ultra vires with the company's objects clause.[4] The objects clause lists the things which the company can do—the company's capacity. If it enters into a transaction not included in the clause, that transaction will be at common law, ultra vires and void. It will be discovered that even where the company has the capacity, a transaction made on its behalf may still not be enforceable against it because the agent who made it had no authority to do so.[5]

As we said when studying the doctrine in the UK, to some scholars like Gower the ultra vires transactions were abolished in relation to the company's capacity, and more specifically about the lack of it when dealing with third parties; nevertheless, the *questio iuris* remains when it is about both the want of powers of directors or an excess of the granted ones. According to one line of British authorities, this is the "new" ultra vires rule, or concretely, the early approach that it had back at the very beginning of the nineteenth century. However, in considering Gower's postulate a call must be done to Directive 2012/30/EU, (2)b that provides: "The statutes or the instrument of incorporation of the company shall always give at least the following information: (…) the objects of the company".[6]

Professor Gower's thought about no longer a provision requiring a company to set up its objects is grounded in such a Directive. This author proclaims that his opinion is based on an interpretation of that provision, as requiring the company's articles to state its objects (if it has them) but not as requiring the company to have objects.[7] From our point of view, it makes no sense to have an objects clause without content. It is clear that legislators made it mandatory to give information concerning

[2] "The validity of an act done by a company shall not be called into question on the ground of lack of capacity by reason of anything in the company's constitution".

[3] Gower et al. (2016), 172–174.

[4] Smith et al. (2016), pp. 96–97.

[5] See footnote 4.

[6] Directive 2012/30/EU, art. 2(b) requires companies to state their objects in the statutes or in the instrument of incorporation and these objects determine the company's capacity. A statement of the company's objects clause may have legal consequences in three ways. Firstly, the directors only have the authority to act within the stated objects. Secondly, the objects are a limitation regarding the rules on representation. Finally, to protect minorities, the directors have a duty to act within the stated objects. Where they do not do so, they may be liable to the minority. The requirement to disclose the objects must be understood in line with this provision. The objects of the company determine the kind of business in which the company can engage. Thus, it is a permanent limitation of the company's business. It may be changed however according to the rules of changing the articles of association. See, Andersen et al. (2017), p. 46.

[7] Gower et al. (2016), p. 173, footnote 89.

company's objects, another thing is that the objects clause allows the firm to perform any kind of legal commercial, or industrial activity.

Anyway, there is no doubt about the intimate connection between the objects clause and the ultra vires doctrine. In the memorandum of association, the objects clause defines the proposed external transactions of the corporation, and the articles of association have to deal with those internal relations that arose between the shareholders and the company. Let us be clear. The ultra vires doctrine is grounded in two scenarios: the corporation's lack of capacity and the want of power of the directors. Therefore, it is rewarding to analyze the influence of the objects clause in the ultra vires, and vice versa.

From a financial perspective, the foundation of a corporation follows an economic purpose consisting in obtaining a financial benefit to divide among the shareholders or what Romans called: *animus lucrandi.* On the other hand, from a legal point of view, the incorporation of a firm is conducted by the will of the individuals involved in the business with a perdurability vocation, and according to the nature of the corporation type depending on the jurisdiction. Thus, the corporation is the outcome of a determined group of individuals' will that cooperate to get involved in a commercial/industrial activity with an *animus lucrandi*, and once it comes into the business environment, it forms a different person from those who created it. In turn, the *affectio societatis* leads individuals to reach a collective interest on behalf of the firm. Once the firm has accomplished the legal requirements, it can get rights, and it is subject to the enforcement of obligations. Because the corporation was created as a legal fiction, it consequently requires legal recognition to be considered as a juristic person.[8]

Thereby, for a corporation to be able to interact in the business world, it is necessary to take account of the commercial goals to get by. Having done this, the laws regulating the corporation and the corporate contract profile the route, allowing the firm to be involved in every kind of lawful industrial or commercial activity, or determining its limits to some specific acts or transactions. This is possible to do it through the objects clause. It is been usually classified the object's clause as *principal* and *complementary* or *ancillary.* The first must describe the chief acts for which the

---

[8] There is certain reluctance in the common law to receive the civil law *fiction theory.* Even more, Pollock is incredulous about their application related to the ultra vires doctrine. He proclaims that may find Lord Selborne saying in 1872 that a railway company "is a mere abstraction of law. All that it does, all that the law imputes to it as its act, must be that which can be legally done within the powers vested in it by law. Consequently, a thing which is ultra vires and unauthorized is not an act of the company in such a sense as that the consent of the company to that act can be pleaded". This might well have been said by a man with his head full of the Fiction theory, and Lord Selborne, though not very learned in the antiquities of the law, may well have known something of the theory in its earlier forms. But the English ultra vires doctrine does not really go back to any ultimate conception as to the nature of a corporate body. It is a doctrine, to use a convenient American term, of constitutional limitations. If the same authority which created a given juristic person, or authorized the constitution of many juristic persons by the performance of certain conditions, has at the same time set bounds to the legal competence of such persons, bounds which are a matter of public knowledge, then acts professedly done in their name and exceeding those bounds are nullities. What we now learn from the history of the ultra vires doctrine, is that in *Ashbury* the House of Lords had an excellent occasion for formally adopting the Fiction Theory if its judicial members had been so minded, and in fact, did not do such thing. See, Pollock (1911), p. 222.

corporation was established, this is continuously executed and may be either exclusive or multiple. With regard to the *complementary* objects, it would all come down to contributing to get the principal object; therefore, the complementary objects must have a direct relationship with the principal.[9]

Alongside the corporation's capacity, the objects clause is the chief item to consider when the ultra vires doctrine comes into effect. In fact, it is contended that both capacity and objects clause form the ultra vires doctrine backbone. It is so, because the blending of the capacity as an attribute of a firm's personality, and the objects clause as a key element of the articles of incorporation, allow to extract and build the set of legal rules around the ultra vires doctrine in corporate law.

As we have taught previously, Latin American, Spanish, and Italian scholars are intellectually curious about this legal topic, and very often have linked the objects clause restrictions to the lack of company capacity. Therefore, taking into account the capacity as an attribute of the personality, the ultra vires rationale inexorably emerges. However, it has been stated that because capacity is an attribute of the personality that cannot be confined by the objects clause, only legal provisions and contract stipulations might do it; nevertheless, shareholders cannot derogate legal provisions, but all those contractual may be. The objects clause as declared in the constitution act not only represents a limit to the directors' powers but also to the corporate capacity. When the shareholders do agree to get involved in a business relationship, besides the legality, safety, and potential revenue for its investment, the objects clause is a fundamental decision criterion and there are many aspects to keep in mind, even moral and religious concerns.[10]

Professor Palmer pointed out that the requisite to delimit the objects clause in the memorandum of association originated in Anglo-American jurisdictions an anomalous practice of "inflated" objects clause describing thoroughly many legal activities that corporations could perform but which they will not necessarily do. Taking into account this phenomenon, a distinction between 'objects' and 'powers' was made. Therefore, to exclude an activity of the ultra vires doctrine, such an act must be directly in connection with the corporate purpose.[11]

On the other hand, the alteration of the objects clause is a crucial aspect to consider in company law because it has a deep repercussion in the corporation's life. In fact, it could trigger disengagement in shareholders who disagree and could even lead to the liquidation of the company. To avoid this undesirable situation, it is been proposed the listing of a broad objects clause that allows the corporation to perform many acts not contemplated at the commencing of their business life. At the same time,

---

[9] For instance, the objects clause could be confined to an exclusive activity such as either the construction of a specific building or the manufacturing, distributing, and selling of clothes. On the other hand, whether the objects clause allows performing multiple acts, usually there is the main activity and another secondary or ancillary but linked to the chief act. However, it is viable that secondary activities do not have a direct relationship to the main, for example, to draft cheques, hire employees, purchase raw material, etc. Vid. Bernal et al. (1991), pp. 29–31.

[10] Caselli (1970), Manovil (1978), pp. 1062–1068, Bernal et al. (1991), pp. 42–50, Colombres (1972), pp. 105–106.

[11] Palmer (1916), p. 66, et seq.

this strategy might contribute to avoiding that the directors incur in ultra vires acts. Conversely, the antithesis advocates the precise determination of the objects clause because this allows protecting the interests of a third party, the shareholders, and even the corporation itself.

Spanish corporate law of July 17, 1951, introduced the distinction between a *shift* in the objects clause (art. 85, num. 4) and the *expansion of operations* (art. 86). The first concept with Italian ascendance and the second from the Swiss Code of Obligations, art. 649.[12] There is a curiosity regarding the significance and scope of these expressions, taking into account that lawmakers remained in silence about the definition of both. To assert that a shift in the objects clause was done, it is necessary to make a complete substitution of the corporate activities. The mere restriction or enlargement of older business activities could not be considered as a shift. Also, it cannot be stated that when there is an amendment in the main activity, consequently there is a shift in the objects clause because it might occur either that it is impossible to determine what the main activity is or that suppression of an ancillary act to the main object could be more relevant to some shareholders that lead them to exercise the recession right. Therefore, there will only be a shift in the objects clause either when there is a radical substitution, or when the original object is broadened or narrowed and the resultant object is objectively diverse.[13]

In some legal systems where the principle of specialty prevails, it is possible to establish in the charters a cumulative number of commercial activities, however, all those provisions must not be as generic or voluminous that they lead to a substantially indeterminate objects clause. This is because it opens the door to subjective interpretations and eventually may frustrate valid business transactions. An example of a

---

[12] Swiss Code of Obligations, art. 649 was repealed by No. 1 of the FA of 4 Oct. 1991, with effect from 1 July 1992 (AS 1992 733; BBl 1983 II 745). However, as a historical background, making a comparison between the Swiss and Spanish regimes there was supremacy in art. 649, because: (i) it allowed the expansion of operations *analogous* to the objects clause provided in the articles of incorporation; (ii) the expansion was possible if the firm has not *overreached* their objects clause; (iii) the agreement could expand the operations, but it was also capable of *narrowing* it; (iv) art. 649 described what must *stand* for expansion. Cf. Broseta (1971), pp. 52–53.

On the other hand, Swiss Code of Obligations, art. 718*a* provides: "(1) The persons with authority to represent the company may carry out any legal acts on behalf of the company that is consistent with the company's objects; and, (2) A restriction of such authority has no effect as against *bona fide* third parties; any provisions governing the exclusive representation of the head office or a branch office or governing joint representation of the company that is entered in the commercial register are exceptions to this rule". Taking into account this provision it seems that Swiss company law admits the principle of specialty; however, denies the validity of the ultra vires doctrine. Vid. Steiger (1973), p. 36.

For a schematic analysis of modern Swiss corporate law, See, Huber-Purtschert (2018), pp. 325–329. As argued in that writing, the provisions of Swiss company law do not provide for the freedom to create any kind of company. Conversely, one's choice is confined to the types of company the law provides for. Most types of business associations are regulated in the Code of Obligations, while more variations can be found in the Civil Code and the Federal Act on Collective Investment Schemes. Which class is chosen in the circumstances depends on the intentions and interests of the people creating the company.

[13] Broseta (1971), pp. 56–58, Garrigues et al. (1953), t. 2, pp. 203–204, Rodríguez (1991), pp. 148–154.

broad legal corporate purpose comes from Colombia's customs law, Decree 1165 of 2019, art. 65, that defines the international trade corporations as:

> Those legal entities whose main corporate purpose is the commercialization and sale of Colombian products abroad, acquired in the domestic market or manufactured by producer partners of the same. Anyway, other activities carried out by the company must always be related to the execution of the main corporate purpose and the economic and financial sustainability of the company.

To delimit the scope of commercial activities of this kind of corporation, the first paragraph provides that the objects clause must indicate the economic sectors with respect to which it will carry out its activity as an international trade corporation.

The objects clause has different roles that reach corporations' deliberations and decisions.[14] In fact, an unconsult variation on it could trigger the exclusion of dissatisfied shareholders. The objects clause is the main course in the memorandum of association menu because both the purposes of the corporation and the powers of directors are contained in it, in such a way that it will allow for knowing the company's capacity and the director's powers in connection with the business operation by both third parties and stockholders. The objects clause must be detailed and carefully crafted, allowing an ordinary individual, an expert corporate law attorney, or a rookie judge easily to understand their content and scope. Thus, anything outside that world represented in the objects clause will be unenforceable, or even better: unlawful. Likewise, In re Thomas v. Railroad Co., 101 U.S. 71, American case law points out:

> The powers of corporations organized under legislative statutes are such, and such only, as those statutes confer. Conceding the rule applicable to all statutes, that what is fairly implied is as much granted as what is expressed, it remains that the charter of a corporation is the measure of its powers and the enumeration of these powers implies the exclusion of all others.

The MBCA–2016 §3.02 provides that: "Unless its articles of incorporation provide otherwise, every corporation has perpetual duration and succession in its corporate name and has the same powers as an individual to do all things necessary or convenient to carry out its business and affairs (…)", and subsequently lists fifteen conducts possible to execute for the directors. This list is not taxative but enunciative. The official comment of this section reads:

> The general philosophy of section 3.02 is that corporations formed under the Act should be automatically authorized to engage in all acts and have all powers that an individual may have. Because broad grants of power of this nature may not be desired in some corporations, section 3.02 generally authorizes articles of incorporation to deny or limit specific powers to a corporation.
>
> The powers of a corporation under the Act exist independently of whether a corporation has a broad or narrow purpose clause. A corporation with a narrow purpose clause nevertheless

[14] For instance, according to Italian C.C. art. 2379, first paragraph, in a joint-stock corporation the deliberations that modify the objects clause by providing for illegal or impossible activities can be contested without time limits. The same prerogative was conferred for limited liability corporations in the C.C. art. 2479-ter, the third paragraph, when the amendments that modify objects clauses stipulate impossible or illegal activities.

> has the same powers as an individual to do all things necessary or convenient to carry out its business. Many actions are therefore within the corporation's powers even if they do not directly affect the limited purpose for which the corporation is formed. For example, a corporation may generally make charitable contributions without regard to the purpose for which the charity will use the funds or may invest money in shares of other corporations without regard to whether the corporate purpose of the other corporation is broader or narrower than the limited purpose clause of the investing corporation. In some instances, however, a limited or narrow purpose clause may be considered to be a restriction on corporate powers as well as a restriction on purposes. Since the same *ultra vires* rule is applicable to corporations that exceed their purposes or powers, it is not necessary to determine whether a narrow purpose clause also limits the powers of the corporation but simply whether the purpose of the transaction in question is consistent with the purpose clause. These issues do not arise in corporations with an 'any lawful business' purpose clause.

Indeed, the objects clause represents the purpose by which the corporation was founded. This purpose is the content of the commercial activity that firms are going to execute throughout their existence, and must be licit. When in the presence of an illicit object clause, the corporate contract is wholly void and cannot be validated or ratified. The corporate contract is a nullity because of an illicit object that can be invoked by a stockholder against another, and by third parties against the corporation. It is disputed if a stockholder or the corporation itself could invoke the nullity against a third party. Even though there is no consensus, the majority of authors consider that if third parties were not cognizant about such illegality they could invoke the nullity to protect their creditors' rights.[15]

References

Andersen P et al (2017) European model companies act

Bernal R et al (1991) Desviaciones del Objeto Social en la Empresa Colombiana. In: Revista de Derecho Comercial, año 24, No. 142 a 144, Buenos Aires

Broseta M (1971) Cambio de Objeto y Ampliación de Operaciones. In: Estudios Jurídicos en Homenaje a Joaquín Garrigues, t. 1, Madrid

Caselli G (1970) Oggetto Sociale e Atti Ultra Vires, Padova

Colombres G (1972) Curso de Derecho Societario, Buenos Aires

Garrigues J et al (1953) Comentario a la Ley de Sociedades Anónimas, t. 1, Madrid

Gower LCB et al (2016) Principles of modern company law, London

Houpin C et al (1935) Traité des Sociétés Comerciales, t. 1, Paris

Huber-Purtschert T (2018) Law of obligations, Zurich

Lyon-Caen Ch, Renault L (1908) Traité de Droit Commercial, t. 2, Paris

Maria P (1906) Les Sociétés Commerciales par Actions, Paris

Manovil R (1978) Actos que Exceden el Objeto Social, Revista de Derecho Comercial, año 11, No. 61 a 66, Buenos Aires

Palmer F (1916) Company law, London

Pollock F (1911) Has the common law received the fiction theory of corporations? L Q Rev 27:219

[15] Lyon-Caen and Renault (1908), pp. 69–76. This author references the evolution of cases involving illicit objects, and how the courts adjudicate them. A thoughtful discussion about the illicit objects clauses in corporate law and the cases related in each one, in Houpin et al. (1935), pp. 115–118.

Rodríguez F (1991) Determinación Estatutaria del Objeto Social. In: Alonso A (coord) Derecho de Sociedades Anónimas, t. 1, Madrid
Sealy L et al (2013) Cases and materials in company law, Oxford
Smith et al (2016) Company law, Harlow
Steiger F (1973) Droit des Sociétés Anonymes en Suisse, Lausanne

Chapter 7
Legal Procedures to Reject Ultra Vires Acts and Transactions

Abstract In this chapter, the legal procedures to reject an ultra vires act or transaction are reviewed. It must be noted that the expression "legal", in the manner used here, has to be understood in a broad sense not limited to a particular judicial action, but also when it has to deal with an administrative procedure to reach such an end. For instance, in some civil law countries, ultra vires acts or transactions can be challenged by either the company or the associates before the courts of justice, administrative agencies, and arbitration tribunals.

To attend to this issue from our comparative perspective, we must point out that there is not a homogeneous procedure to reject an ultra vires act or transaction, neither a specific individual nor a juristic person legitimated to do it and the chosen way varies in each jurisdiction. In fact, the ultra vires doctrine has come to be alleged even in labor law trials.[1] However, taking into account the two main legal systems referred to in this writing—i.e., common law and civil law—we will consider an integral treatment of the *questio iuris* from a dual view. Therefore, we are going to undertake the study grouping all the similar legal families.

Furmston states that there is no authority deciding whether a contracting party can set up ultra vires against a company other than the decision in *Anglo Overseas Agencies Ltd. v. Green*.[2] It may be opportune to consider what answer is dictated on principle. Professor Gower suggests that normal principles of contract law would point against the other contracting party being able to set up ultra vires. This point is not developed but it would seem that he has in mind a case such as infancy, where

[1] In the case of Cucci v. New York City Off-Track Betting Corp. 818 F.Supp. 647, 657–658 (S.D.N.Y.1993), the plaintiff contended that she had been fired as an employee of the defendant in violation of the statutory provisions regulating the defendant and that therefore her firing was ultra vires. This argument was rejected by the court on the ground that the doctrine of ultra vires as embodied in the New York Business Corporation Law §203, could be invoked only by a shareholder or by that state through its attorney-general and not by an employee. Vid. Hamilton (2005), pp. 226–227.

[2] Furmston (1961), p. 717.

M. A. Jiménez Sánchez, *The Ultra Vires Doctrine in Corporate Law*,
SpringerBriefs in Law, https://doi.org/10.1007/978-3-030-88838-1_7

the infant's incapacity is said to be a personal privilege and cannot be relied upon by the other party.[3]

The ancient American case law has ruled:

> A contract of a corporation, which is *ultra vires*, in the proper sense, that is to say, outside the object of its creation as defined in the law of its organization, and therefore beyond the powers conferred upon it by the legislature, is not voidable only, but wholly void, and of no legal effect. The objection to the contract is, not merely that the corporation ought not to have made it, but that it could not make it. The contract cannot be ratified by either party, because it could not have been authorized by either (…) when the contract is beyond the powers conferred upon it by existing laws, neither the corporation, nor the other party to the contract, can be estopped, by assenting to it, or by acting upon it, to show that it was prohibited by those laws.[4]

According to MBCA–2016 §3.04(b) official comment, this section permits challenges to the corporation's lack of power in three cases[5]:

> (i) In a suit by a shareholder against the corporation to enjoin an *ultra vires* act. This suit, however, is subject to the requirements of section 3.04(c). Section 3.04(c) authorizes a court to enjoin or set aside an *ultra vires* act or grant other relief that may be necessary to protect the interests of all affected persons, including the interests of third persons who deal with the corporation. Under this subsection an *ultra vires* act may be enjoined only if all "affected parties" are parties to the suit. The requirement that the action be "equitable" generally means that only third persons dealing with a corporation while specifically aware that the corporation's action was *ultra vires* will be enjoined. The general phrase "if equitable" is used because of the possibility that other circumstances may exist in which it may be equitable to refuse to enforce an *ultra vires* contract. Further, if enforcement of the contract is enjoined, either the third person or the corporation may in the discretion of the court be awarded damages from the other for loss (excluding anticipated profits).

Greenfield points out that the key implication for the corporate practice of an ultra vires doctrine for unlawful acts is that injunctive relief would be available.[6] As when the ultra vires doctrine was more vibrant, individual shareholders could sue to enjoin the corporation from engaging in ultra vires acts, even if such acts were expected to be profitable. Such a right would belong, as it did previously, to each

---

[3] In the opinion of Ballantine (1930), p. 290, an excess of corporate power can be questioned only by a person whose interests are in some way affected. The ultra vires doctrine can be invoked only at the instance of the state, the corporation, its stockholders or creditors whose rights are infringed, or the other party to a contract who is affected by the lack of corporate authority. Not every ultra vires act is ground for forfeiture in quo warranto unless the public interest is threatened.

According to Tit. 28, U.S. Code Judiciary and Judicial Procedure §1695: "Process in a stockholder's action on behalf of his corporation may be served upon such corporation in any district where it is organized or licensed to do business or is doing business". The phrase "is organized or licensed to do business or is doing business" was substituted for the words "resides or is found" as more specific and to conform to section 1391.

[4] 139 U.S. 24 at 59; 35 L.Ed. 55 at 68 (1890).

[5] www.americanbar.org/content/dam/aba/administrative/business_law/corplaws/2016_mbca.authcheckdam.pdf [last accessed: 12/Sept/2021].

[6] Greenfield (2001), p. 1352.

shareholder individually and could be exercised even though every other shareholder was opposed.[7]

> (ii) In a suit by the corporation, either directly or through a legal representative, against incumbent or former officers or directors for authorizing or causing the corporation to engage in an *ultra vires* act. Again, this section does not address whether there is liability for causing the corporation to enter into an *ultra vires* act; it simply preserves the power of the corporation to assert that certain corporate action was *ultra vires*.

These provisions mean that not only can a shareholder bring an injunctive action to stop a corporation from acting unlawfully, but it can also sue the responsible corporate officials in a derivative action to recover any losses to the corporation. Thus, while a shareholder can sue to enjoin a corporation from breaking the law if the illegality is ongoing or has yet to occur if the illegality is in the past, the proper remedy is a damages action.[8]

> (iii) In a suit by the attorney general under section 14.30. This provision does not answer the question whether a corporation may be dissolved or enjoined by the attorney general for provision.

The ultra vires doctrine would differ from the doctrine of fiduciary duty in that it would provide the incorporating state, through its attorney general, some powerful remedies. Traditionally, because the charter limited the power of the corporation and because keeping corporations within such limitations was important to the state, the state retained two important enforcement mechanisms. The first was the power to enjoin a wayward corporation's ultra vires acts. Second, a corporation's ultra vires acts furnished the state "a ground for the forfeiture of the charter of the corporation, or for ousting it from the exercise of the unauthorized powers, upon the state's application in a quo warranto proceeding".[9]

Professor Hamilton remembrances the following case.[10] In Tallahatchie Valley Elec. Power Ass'n v. Miss. Propane Gas Ass'n, 812 So.2 912, Util. L. Rep. P 26,803 (Miss. 2002), Miss. Propane, a trade association representing manufacturers of propane gas, sued Tallahatchie Power (hereinafter, TVEPA) when TVEPA began selling propane gas. TVEPA was organized pursuant to state and federal statutory provisions designed to encourage the dissemination of electric energy. The Mississippi Supreme Court held that TVEPA had exceeded its statutory authority when it acquired a subsidiary that sold propane gas. TVEPA then argued that the lawsuit brought against it by the Gas Association was essentially an ultra vires action, and that the plaintiffs, therefore, lacked standing to bring a lawsuit claiming that corporate action is ultra vires. The Mississippi Supreme Court agreed that the lawsuit involved an ultra vires claim because it challenged TVEPA's power to act pursuant to statutory and its corporate charter. However, it held that the association nevertheless had standing because it was a trade group that represented companies that

---

[7] See footnote 6.

[8] Greenfield (2001), p. 1357.

[9] Greenfield (2001), p. 1359.

[10] Hamilton (2005), p. 226.

were shareholders in TVEPA. On the merits, the Court refused to enjoin TVEPA's subsidiary's sales of non-electric energy products such as propane gas, even though this line of business was ultra vires for TVEPA. The Court reasoned that the members of the association had no "legal right to be free of the lawful competition posed by" TVEPA's subsidiary, and concluded that the association did not assert any "legally cognizable injury upon which the relief sought may be granted". The Court held that TVEPA's ownership of the subsidiary violated state statutes, but that the competition that its subsidiary was engaging in was lawful. The Court noted that the subsidiary was a separate legal entity, legally distinct from its parent. Thus, it appears that while TVEPA broke the law by acquiring a subsidiary that was engaged in a business that the parent could not lawfully engage in, the subsidiary did not violate the law because it was engaged in what was, for it (though not for its corporate partner), a legal competitive enterprise.[11]

In turn, Smith proclaims that the company should not carry out acts or enter into transactions which are beyond the company's objects clause, and a shareholder, upon discovering the intention of the company's directors to enter into such an agreement, may obtain an injunction so as to prevent it from going ahead (though not if it has already been ratified by way of a special resolution of the general meeting).[12] However, it should be noted that if the transaction has already been carried out, the shareholder may only seek to gain damages from the wrongdoer directors for the company. It is also worth pointing out at this stage that if a director has exceeded his powers then this may be taken as a breach of the terms of his contract of employment as well as a breach of his directors' duties; CA 2006 s. 171 imposes a duty on directors to abide by the company's constitution.[13]

On the other hand, in civil law countries the ultra vires acts or transactions can be challenged by either the company or the associates before the courts and even in some jurisdictions before administrative agencies, and arbitration tribunals. In fact, there are legislations where in accordance with the type of company, such as the SAS, there are special procedures. Indeed, following similar roots, civil law countries usually have a standard judicial procedure through which the plaintiff sues against the defendant looking for the invalidity of the ultra vires act or transaction.

As we said before, the ultra vires acts or transactions do not have validity because they are considered a lack of company capacity, in as much as the company's capacity is confined to the commercial and industrial activities described in their objects clause. In consequence, as a general principle, all those acts and transactions executed beyond the objects clause are wholly void because of the want of capacity. However, the new provisions of the French Civil Code enacted by Ordonnance No. 2016-131, lays out in art. 1145:

> Every natural person is able to conclude a contract, except in the case of lack of capacity provided for by legislation.

---

[11] See footnote 10.

[12] Smith et al. (2016), p. 97.

[13] See footnote 12.

> The capacity of legal persons is limited to acts useful for realizing their purpose as defined by their statutes and acts which are incidental to them, in accordance with the rules applicable to each of those persons.

In turn, art. 1147 ibid. provides that a lack of capacity to conclude a contract is a ground of *relative nullity*. In consequence, following this brand new rule, an ultra vires act will be affected by relative nullity. Conversely to French law, in Italy and Spain, an ultra vires act is not relative nullity but voidable. Indeed, Italian C.C. art. 1425, points out that the contract will be *voidable* if one part is legally incapable of making the contract. Thus, this provision has led to hold that taking into account the contractual nature of the corporate contract—i.e., plurilateral contract—then ultra vires acts and transactions in the form of contract will be voidable, and not just wholly void. The same can be said in Spain, following C.C. art. 1300,[14] which allows deducing that the lack of capacity leads to the act or transaction to be *annulled*.

In Latin American countries such as Colombia, the objects clause was conceived as a limit to the company's capacity, in consequence, any act or transaction beyond or outside of this scope becomes ultra vires. Thus, any decision adopted by the general meeting or the board beyond or outside of this limit is an absolute nullity.[15] Notwithstanding, Argentinean law also conceives the ultra vires act as a lack of company capacity, however, it does not lay out their legal consequence, specifically the Civil Code does not enlist the cases when an act is relative nullity or absolute nullity. In that respect, there is a vibrant controversy; however, the predominant thesis is that such kinds of acts or transactions either beyond or outside the capacity is a relative nullity.[16]

Finally, as a general rule, when the directors execute an ultra vires act or transaction the company is bound to comply with it; nevertheless, the company has an action at law against the directors to recover the damages caused to the firm because of their intentional or negligent behavior. This action at law often has a civil procedure according to the judicial or administrative procedure.[17]

---

[14] Spanish C.C. art. 1300: "Contracts which meet the requirements expressed in article 1261 may be annulled, even if there is no injury to the contracting parties, provided that they suffer from any defects which invalidate them in accordance with the law". According to art. 1261, ibid.: "There is no contract unless the following requirements are present: (1) Consent of the contracting parties. (2) A certain object which is the subject matter of the agreement. (3) Cause of the obligation established".

[15] Gil (2010), p. 235. According to Colombian C.C. art. 1742, the absolute nullity is able and should be declared by the judge even ex officio, when it clearly appears in the act or contract; also it can be alleged for any individual interested in it, by the Public Ministry in the interest of the moral or of the law. When the absolute nullity is not originated due to an illicit object or an illicit cause, it can be ratified by the parts, and in any case, can be validated by the extraordinary prescription.

[16] Cf. Cifuentes (2004), pp. 766–783.

[17] French C.Co. art. L. 223–22, and L. 225–251; Italian C.C. art. 2393; Spanish Decree 1/2010, art. 238; Argentinean Law 19.550 of 1972, art. 274; Brazilian Law 6.404 of 1976, art. 158, 159; Colombian Law 222 of 1995, art. 24 and 25; Mexican General Law of Corporations of 1934, art. 161; Peruvian Law 26887 of 1997, art. 12.

References

Ballantine H (1930) Manual of corporation law, Chicago
Cifuentes S (2004) Negocio Jurídico, Buenos Aires
Furmston MP (1961) Who can plead that a contract is ultra vires? Modern Law Rev 24
Gil J (2010) Impugnación de Decisiones Societarias, Bogotá
Greenfield K (2001) Ultra vires lives! Virginia Law Rev 87(7)
Hamilton R et al (2005) Corporations, St. Paul
Smith et al (2016) Company law, Harlow

Chapter 8
Ratification of Ultra Vires Acts and Transactions

Abstract In this final chapter, the different ways to ratify an ultra vires act or transaction are taught. Likewise, the legitimated person to make it. To the extent that in ancient times there were no legislative provisions related to this issue, judges and courts have delivered many opinions some of them contradictory.

As a general rule, the acts or contracts in excess of the charter of a corporation are ultra vires, and therefore not binding upon the company, yet, after a corporation has enjoyed the benefit of an act performed on its behalf, it will be estopped, when charged with responsibility on account of the act, from setting up as a defense that the transaction was ultra vires. However, Morawetz considers this statement inaccurate, taking into account that principles of the law of agency apply to corporations, and a person does not become responsible for acts performed in his name merely because the acts have accrued to his benefit. Thus, a person may become responsible for them ratifying it, but ratification would imply an intention to adopt the unauthorized act. Ratification by a corporation of an act beyond its charter means ratification by the entire body of shareholders; thus, no agent of a corporation has authority to ratify an act which he had not the original authority to do.[1]

The distinction between the defense of ultra vires and the defense of lack of agent's authority is often misunderstood. The ultra vires statutes merely confirm that a corporation has the capacity of a real person. The corporation's authority may be limited by provisions in its articles or by common law rules. For example, common law doctrines establish that the act of directors in conveying corporate property for

[1] Morawetz (1886), vol. 2, §581. In accordance with the predominant opinion, there can be no ratification of an illegal transaction that will render it enforceable. In re Cartwright v. Albuquerque Hotel Co., 36 N.M. 189, 11 P.(2d) 261 (1932); Runcie v. Corn Exchange Bank Trust Co., 6 N.Y.S.(2d) 616 (1938); Baird v. McDaniel Printing Co., 25 Tenn. App. 144, 148, 153 S.W.(2d) 135, 138 (1941), in which the court pointed out: "Corporate transactions which are illegal because prohibited by statute are void, and cannot support an action nor become enforceable by performance, ratification, or estoppel." 35. La. Act 250 of 1928, §12, I [Dart's Stats. (1939) §1092, I]. In *Runcie*, it was held that shareholders could not ratify ultra vires acts. In turn, in *Ashbury* it was submitted that: "Where there could be no mandate, there cannot be any ratification".

M. A. Jiménez Sánchez, *The Ultra Vires Doctrine in Corporate Law*, SpringerBriefs in Law, https://doi.org/10.1007/978-3-030-88838-1_8

no consideration, or for woefully inadequate consideration, may not be ratified by less than unanimous shareholder action. Many courts describe such gifts or wasteful acts as ultra vires. No such act can be in furtherance of corporate purposes unless ratified by all shareholders, and, thus, such act is beyond the corporation's power. However, for a case holding both that a guaranty issue without authority is ultra vires and that the corporation cannot assert either an ultra vires defense or a lack of officer authority defense.[2]

According to Black's Law Dictionary the second significance of the word *ratification* is "conformation and acceptance of a previous act, thereby making the act valid from the moment it was done".[3] This is the most accurate meaning of ratification in the context of this writing. According to every jurisdiction the ultra vires acts or transactions are nonexistent, wholly void, voidable, relativity nullity, etc., because of the lack of capacity. Beyond the legal adverse consequences, it is appropriate to inquire about the possibility to ratify such acts or transactions, taking as a starting point an explicit deal or tacit conduct on behalf of the corporation or the third party.

The first approach upon this subject matter teaches that a company may ratify a contract which it has the power to make. Hence, if a contract is entered into by someone on its behalf without authority, or is voidable because some formality has not been observed, it may be ratified by the corporation acting in some proper form. Thus, a voidable contract may be ratified by a majority of the stockholders because a majority having control of the corporation within the general scope of its powers might have made the original contract. But an ultra vires contract, due to excess of the corporate power cannot be ratified.[4]

In *Central Transportation Co. v. Pullman's Car Co.* Justice Gray, in delivering the opinion of the Court said:

> A contract of a corporation, which is *ultra vires* (...) outside the object of its creation as defined in the law of its organization, and therefore beyond the powers conferred upon it by the legislature, is not voidable only, but wholly void, and of no legal effect. The objection to the contract is, not merely that the corporation ought not to have made it, but that it could not make it. *The contract cannot be ratified by either party, because it could not have been authorized by either*. No performance on either side can give the unlawful contract any validity, or be the foundation of any right of action upon it.[5] (italics added)

---

[2] O'Kelley et al. (2010), p. 688. In re Inter. Corp. v. Moody, 411 S.W.2d 578 (Tex. Civ. App. 1966).

[3] Garner (2009), p. 1376. Civil Law scholars stand for *ratification* as the unilateral act through which one individual or moral person, takes charge of both rights and obligations of a business done on behalf of it by someone to whom he had not conferred power or beyond the powers granted. See, Capitant (1966), p. 459.

[4] Elliott (1911), §221. There is must be noted that in *Ashbury* the contract for the purchase of a concession for building a railway was declared ultra vires, and consequently void. In this case, not even the subsequent assent of the whole body of shareholders could ratify it. In *Tippecanoe Co. v. Lafayette, et al. 50 Ind. 85 (1875)* it was ruled that: "A contract ultra vires the charter is void, and cannot be made valid by any subsequent act of the corporation, because there is no residuary power to confirm it. What they could not make, they cannot confirm. A void act can never become valid, merely because it remains unquestioned".

[5] Central Transportation Co. v. Pullman Palace Car Co., 139 U.S. 24 (1890). In California Bank v. Kennedy, 167 U.S. 362, a certificate for shares of the stock of corporation M was issued in the name

The ratification of an ultra vires act is something widely discussed, taking as a starting point the possibility of amendments to the objects clause. If the analysis concludes in a positive answer, consequently it may be ratified. When in presence of an anomalous act due to an excess of the granted powers, the natural or juristic person directly prejudiced might declare its will to remedy the situation, in this case, it will be the shareholders and subsidiarity the corporation.

Indeed, the ultra vires doctrine has a double scope in protecting both company creditors and shareholder patrimony. In ancient English company law, it was submitted that though not warranted by the deed of settlement, would be valid whether it was either previously authorized or subsequently ratified by all the shareholders.[6] The underlying rationale has to deal with the fact that if the shareholders unanimously adhere to such directors' act, then the powers granted are extended and consequently the company's capacity too.[7] An ultra vires contract may become binding by the ratification, assent, or acquiescence of all the shareholders, according to some courts, but not according to others unless the public or the creditors are prejudicially affected. The doctrine is laid down by certain jurisdictions that ultra vires acts cannot be ratified so as to validate them even by the unanimous assent of all the stockholders. This would seem to be erroneous on principle, at least so far as the defense is urged for the benefit or protection of the stockholders, which is the principal object rather than the interest of the public or the creditors.[8]

In the early days, the English ultra vires doctrine and their subsequent developments were so strict, that even if the shareholders would like to ratify such acts performed beyond the objects clause, they were not able to do it. This issue was overcome in 1948, allowing corporations to shift the objects clause through a reform of the articles of incorporation.

---

of corporation X, and dividends thereon were paid into the treasury of X. M became insolvent, and a creditor sought to enforce against X the liability attaching to shareholders in M. The court allowed X to defend, on the ground that the purchase of the shares by X was ultra vires. "It would be a contradiction in terms to assert that there was a total want of power by any act to assume the liability, and yet to say that by a particular act the liability resulted. *The transaction being absolutely void, could not be confirmed or ratified*" (italics added). Some criticism about this reasoning in Warren (1910), pp. 497, 504.

[6] Spackman v. Evans, 3 HL 171 (1868).

[7] The Companies Act 1862 expressly prohibited an alteration of the objects clause in the memorandum of association, even with the unanimous consent of all the shareholders.

[8] Ballantine (1930), pp. 282–283. The consent of the shareholders need not be expressed by any formal vote of authorization or ratification. Where the funds of the corporation are openly employed in a venture outside the contemplated scope of corporate action, so that the fact could upon inquiry be ascertained, if the shareholder does not restrain the further prosecution of the venture within a reasonable time, it is proper for the law to impose upon him ratification of such employment. If shareholders are to be protected, to the detriment of outsiders, against the unauthorized acts of the directors and officers, it is not improper to impose a duty upon shareholders to inquire as to the conduct of the directors and officers, and to restrain such conduct, if improper. Cf. Warren (1910), p. 537, footnote 4.

In the opinion of De La Cámara, the acts beyond the objects clause are not by themselves void.[9] It seems evident that whether the shareholders either majority or unanimously can shift the objects clause, they also could ratify any act beyond it. Such an act will be lawful ab initio if the directors either have previously consulted and obtained the general meeting's approbation, or the act was latterly ratified. Thus, this is a typical scenario of roman aphorism: *qui potest plus, potest minus.*[10]

As we said, the new French C.C. art. 1147 provides that a lack of capacity to conclude a contract is a ground of *relative nullity*. In consequence, an ultra vires act will be affected by a relative nullity and could be ratified taking into account the following rules: (i) the act must be affected by the relative nullity; (ii) the author of the ratification must have specific knowledge about the vice that affects the act and the intention of correcting it; (iii) the ratification must be effective in a moment when there are not such vices.[11] Finally, the ratification could be either express or tacit. It is tacit when there is knowledge about the vice and the intention to ratify it. On the contrary, talking about the express ratification, C.C. art. 1338, lays out:

> An act confirming or ratifying an obligation against which the law admits an action for nullity or rescission, is only valid when it contains within it the substance of such obligation, mention of the motive for the action for rescission, and an intention to remedy the defect on which such action was founded.
>
> Failing such act of confirmation or ratification, it is sufficient that the obligation is executed voluntarily after the period at which the obligation may be validly confirmed or ratified.
>
> Confirmation, ratification, or voluntary execution, in the forms and at the period determined by the law, imports renunciation of the arguments and exceptions which may be opposed to such act, without prejudice nevertheless to the right of third persons.

In Latin America the Mexican C.C. art. 1795 lays out that the contract can be invalidated because of the want of legal capacity of both parts, or just one of them. In turn, according to art. 2230 ibid. the nullity due to the lack of capacity can only be invoked by the incapable. When the contract is a nullity because of the lack of capacity, it can be ratified when the vice or motive of such nullity is over, and there is no other cause that invalidates the ratification (art. 2233). In turn, Colombian C.Co. art. 844, contemplates a general rule about the ratification of ultra vires acts and transactions. Indeed, according to such norm, the ratification of the interested party, if it is done with the same formalities that the law requires for the ratified business, will have retroactive effect, except insofar as it damages the rights of third parties.

In Argentina, Manóvil claims that except in the case of any unlawful act or a regulated commercial activity by the government, any kind of act executed beyond the corporation's powers only concern the shareholders, consequently they can ratify it by unanimity.[12] On the other hand, Halperin and Cabanellas state that taking into account Law 19.550, art. 58, any act "notoriously foreign" to the objects clause

---

[9] De La Cámara (1977), p. 332.

[10] The antithesis holds that the general meeting has no legitimation to ratify an act not described in the objects clause because it is also bound by the company's purpose. Cf. La Villa (1996), p. 339.

[11] Mazeaud et al. (1960), p. 346. An extensive analysis about this topic in Japiot (1909), pp. 564–582.

[12] Manóvil (1978), p. 1068.

cannot be approved or ratified by the general meeting because it is not an issue about a lack of authorization to perform them, but an excess of imputation frame of the conducts of the company's members as part of the company's organs, regardless the procedure to decide and execute such acts. Not even the later modification of the by-laws could be possible because the objects clause is not retroactive.[13] In turn, Italian authors such as Galgano consider that the acts executed without authorization are not wholly void but only ineffective, and if the authorization is given latterly—i.e., ratified—the act will be effective ex tunc.[14]

Lastly, Brazilian C.C. art. 662, provides that acts performed by those who do not have a mandate or have it without powers sufficient are ineffective in relation to the one in whose name they were practiced unless it ratifies them. Ratification must be expressed, or result from an unambiguous act, and will retroact to the date of the act. In turn, art. 665 ibid. lays out that the mandatary who exceeds the powers of the mandate, or proceeds against them, will be considered a mere business manager, as long as the mandator does not ratify the acts.

References

Ballantine H (1930) Manual of corporation law, Chicago

Cabanellas G (1993) Derecho Societario, t. 2, Buenos Aires

Capitant H (1966) Vocabulario Jurídico, Buenos Aires

De La Cámara M (1977) Estudios de Derecho Mercantil, vol 1, Jaén

Elliott C (1911) The law of private corporations, Indianapolis

Galgano F (1969) Persone Giuridiche, Bologna

Garner B (2009) Black's law dictionary, St. Paul

Halperin I (1958) Manual de Sociedades Anónimas, Buenos Aires

Japiot R (1909) Nullités en Matiére d'actes Juridiques, Paris

La Villa G (1996) Introduzione al Diritto Europeo delle Societa, Torino

Manóvil R (1978) Actos que Exceden el Objeto Social. In: Revista de Derecho Comercial, año 11, No. 61 a 66, Buenos Aires

Mazeaud H et al (1960) Lecciones de Derecho Civil, pt. 2, vol 1, Buenos Aires

Messineo F (1971) Derecho Civil y Comercial, t. 2, Buenos Aires

Morawetz V (1886) Treatise on the law of private corporations, vol 2, Boston

O'Kelley C et al (2010) Corporations and other business associations, New York

Warren E (1910) Executory ultra vires transactions. Harvard Law Rev 24

[13] Halperin (1958), p. 426, Cabanellas (1993), p. 308.

[14] Galgano (1969), p. 228. The company through the general meeting could ratify an ultra vires act taking into account that Italian C.C. art. 1399, the first paragraph allows it. Nevertheless, it seems that the ratification must be express, and not only tacit. Vid. Messineo (1971), pp. 428–430.

Chapter 9
Conclusions

The ultra vires doctrine is mainly concerned about the fact that corporations can only pursue the purposes for which they were created, and any kind of act or transaction beyond this point becomes ultra vires, and consequently, void. An ultra vires act or transaction does not necessarily imply an illegal behavior; it is all about acting beyond the corporate capacity. In other words, if the corporation tries to effect purposes other than those for which it was created, its acts or transactions will be ultra vires. Another subsequent variant of the doctrine teaches that the company's directors have confined powers granted in the articles of association and legal provisions. Thereby when the directors perform an act for which they do not have authority, such act or transaction becomes ultra vires.

Some criticism about the ultra vires doctrine is the lack of practical application, taking into account that anomalies that arose from the excess of power can be resolved with the legal mechanism in accordance with the specific business transaction involved in it, such as the law of contract or negotiable instruments. Thus, the rules affecting each one of those subject matters must come into effect making the use of the ultra vires doctrine unnecessary.

The ultra vires doctrine in civil law jurisdictions such as Italy, France, Spain, Argentina, Brasil, Colombia, and México has plenty of validity taking into account the principle of specialty (*spécialité statutaire*). However, it is discussed in Germany because the law equates the juristic persons' capacity to human beings, in that respect, the corporations have a full capacity to perform a broad range of commercial and industrial acts and transactions, without incurring in an ultra vires business.

In all those countries where the doctrine applies, there is not a homogeneous procedure to reject an ultra vires act or transaction, nor is there a specific natural or juristic person authorized to do it and the chosen way will depend on each jurisdiction. The same can be said about their legal consequences (wholly nullity, voidable, relative nullity, etc.) and the ratification mechanism, where it is allowed.

M. A. Jiménez Sánchez, *The Ultra Vires Doctrine in Corporate Law*,
SpringerBriefs in Law, https://doi.org/10.1007/978-3-030-88838-1_9

The manufacturer's authorised representative in the EU is Springer Nature Customer Service Centre GmbH, Europaplatz 3, 69115 Heidelberg, Germany. If you have any concerns regarding our products, please contact ProductSafety@springernature.com

Printed and bound by CPI Group (UK) Ltd, Croydon, CR0 4YY
30/09/2026
02225708-0008